LIFE AMPLIFIED

T0208884

LIFE AMPLIFIED

OUR FAMILY TOUCHED BY AUTISM

Karen Skogen Haslem

authorHOUSE®

AuthorHouse™
1663 Liberty Drive
Bloomington, IN 47403
www.authorhouse.com
Phone: 1 (800) 839-8640

Published by AuthorHouse 03/18/2015

ISBN: 978-1-5049-0123-9 (sc)
ISBN: 978-1-5049-0342-4 (e)

Library of Congress Control Number: 2015904086

Print information available on the last page.

Any people depicted in stock imagery provided by Thinkstock are models, and such images are being used for illustrative purposes only. Certain stock imagery © Thinkstock.

This book is printed on acid-free paper.

CONTENTS

DEDICATION

*This book is dedicated to Our Lord Jesus who came up with
the plan of blessing us with a son who happens to have autism
and sending us on the adventure of this life with him.
Also to the many people who have walked alongside our son through
the years. It's impossible to name each of them, but we want to
acknowledge the dedicated people who spent the greatest amount of
time with him. Our son is the amazing young man he is today due in
part to your care and dedication. Thank you is simply not enough.*

*Teacher Tiffani Tuscherer, Kyle Smith, Teacher Wendy
Mrs. Hudock, Teacher Gayle Haydon, Miss Julia
Dr. Rob Dramov, Sherry McDonald
Mr. Ranslow, Jacque Hallquist
Mrs. Watters, Lisa Proffit
Mr. Jones, Mrs. Jones, Cliff Tunner, Susan Dieter Robinson, Mary Flagg
Jill Hertel, Janelle Mayo, Josh Kauffman, Brooke Harris
DeAna Aust, Nancy Donar
Mrs. Makebish, Miss Gohring, Ms. April*

CHAPTER 1

From Infertility to Placement Day

Aaron got there first. First to the place you reach in your heart and mind where adoption becomes an opportunity. We had spent more time in the doctor's office that day, this time hearing about needles, the calendar, and the expense of in-vitro fertilization. Money was tight. Aaron was in college full time working towards his engineering degree. We both worked full time jobs to avoid any school loan debt after his graduation. The $25K price tag on having a baby who had our genes was just not in the budget. We had been trying to have a baby for almost 5 years; the last year spent on and off Clomid, a popular infertility drug at the time. For months I had hoped and prayed that this would finally be "the month" and I could finally have that moment a woman dreams about, and I could tell Aaron he was going to be a daddy. It never came and I would cry myself to sleep wondering why God would put this deep desire to be a mommy in my being.

Like I said, Aaron got there first. He was so very gentle and patient and waited for me to get to that same place. One night he reminded me that my favorite book as a child, entitled *The Family Nobody Wanted*, was about a family who adopted 12 children. Now of course I didn't want 12. Just one little someone to fill our house with pitter-patters and fingerprints. I had to come to the realization that God had a plan that was better than my plan. I had to trust Him above anything else and let go of my ideal family. I submitted my plan to God and honestly said "your will, not mine." At that moment I had no idea how incredible God's plan was for us.

We walked into the adoption agency on a brisk January day. Our social worker was a lovely woman who chatted with us about all the ins and outs of the adoption process through their private Christian agency. We chose a private agency even though we knew it would be more expensive than adopting a child through the state. We chose this particular agency because they provided counseling for young women before, during, and most importantly after the adoption. We had the choice to pursue a domestic or international adoption. For us the higher cost of an international adoption in addition to all the travel expenses was not an option. We also knew that there were so many children born right here in the states that needed a home. Another reason that we chose this particular agency was that they arranged what are called "semi-open adoptions." A semi-open adoption is one where everyone is on a first name basis; a young woman, also known as a birth mother, is able to have arranged contact with the family after the adoption, all terms agreed upon before the baby is even born. We felt that this was especially important for us. We really wanted our birth mom to be well taken care of and supported throughout the process. At the time, I could only imagine how hard it would be for a woman to hand over her precious baby. She would make such a sacrifice to give us such a gift.

As with any adoption, the paperwork was daunting: background checks, fingerprinting, and 150 personal questions about us. The questions ranged from where and when were we were born all the way to how we planned to discipline our child in his teen years. The questions took much thought and countless hours to answer. One particularly memorable form was about children with special needs. The form listed about 40 different disabilities and birth defects such as blindness, cleft palate, heart murmur, and Down's syndrome. We thought carefully as we answered each one. We wanted a baby. We wanted the baby that God hand picked. The little one that He had in mind may not be perfect in the world's eyes but we knew that God doesn't make mistakes. As we went through the list we decided to rule out the disabilities that would have been difficult for us to care for financially. For instance, a baby that would need several heart surgeries was not one we felt we could provide the proper care for, financially. It was at this point that we learned that a mixed race baby was considered special needs because they are harder to place. We really didn't care what color our baby was. We just wanted to start our family.

Soon after all our initial paperwork was complete, I got a call from our social worker who told us we had been approved. This was a big deal for me; it was like the doctor telling me I was pregnant. I so wanted to make the moment special as I told my husband, much like I had imagined I would telling him I was pregnant. I left work early and went on a mission, shopping for little baby shoes. Up until this time I had tried to stay away from the baby section in stores, it would just make me sad and I'd end up crying all the way home. But on this day a baby in our future was inevitable. I went to several stores until I found the perfect pair: a tiny pair of red Converse sneakers, a pair that would work for a baby boy or a baby girl. I wrapped them up in a sweet little white box and tied them with a white bow. I attached a little note that said:

"Congratulations! We're approved ! You're going to be a Daddy!"

My husband's lackluster reaction was not what I had imagined all those years, but my vision of motherhood had been turned on it's head already, so it mattered little.

Aaron: What can I say? I am an engineer. I study the practical application of things. In my mind, we were approved, but not yet chosen. At that moment, there was an untold amount of time that it could take before we were even considered candidates by a birth mom. Which to me meant we could be years away from actually becoming parents. I couldn't bring myself to get excited over being approved. Even after being chosen by a birth mom, it was possible that she could change her mind and chose someone else. I had reserved myself to being excited at the moment I put MY baby into the backseat of my car and drove away with MY family. Besides, who would have doubted that we would be approved? We were shoo-ins for that.

Near the end of our adoption process we were required to attend 6 weeks of adoption classes in a group setting with other hopeful couples. During this time, in March of that year, I woke up with some strange pains. After I spoke to my OBGYN, he had me come in for an exam and a blood test. The tests showed that I was pregnant but that something was wrong. At first they thought I had been carrying twins and had lost one but it turned out that a baby was growing in my fallopian tube. I had to have a surgery to take out the tube before it ruptured. At the follow-up appointment, the doctor spoke some infamous words: "During the surgery I discovered that your ovaries are covered with cysts, which explains why you have such a difficult time getting pregnant. Now with one tube gone, your chances are very slim. *The chances of you having a baby are one in a million. You have a better chance of winning the lottery.*"

I was devastated and had to go through the grieving process all over again. I was questioning God once again about His plan. I knew it was a good plan but it sure didn't feel like it. I grieved the baby, whom we named Sasha, that we had lost. I remember people saying things like "well, at least you weren't very far along" and "there must have been something wrong with that baby" and "God knows best." People meant well but I was crushed inside. For me it was the death of my child. I had lost a child that I wasn't allowed to grieve socially. I couldn't bury that baby. There was no memorial service. I didn't even get to see a little face. I was angry and felt cheated. In my grief, God allowed me to be honest. I know He counted every tear and felt my heartache. He and my sweet husband allowed me to grieve. Soon enough I had peace again and we went forward with our plans to adopt.

Our adoption process was almost complete. Our last task was writing the letter to the birth mother. Each waiting couple was required to write a letter to a potential birth mom. An important part of the process for women wanting to place their baby up for adoption was that they got to choose the parents for their baby with help from their social worker. The social worker would choose a few couples and pass the handful of letters on to the birth mom. A letter written to a birth mom would be several pages long and include various photographs. Couples would write a brief history about themselves, about their relationship, their reasons for wanting to adopt, and their hopes and dreams for the future. The letter was her glimpse into the life her child would have. We spent two weeks preparing ours, carefully choosing photographs and heartfelt words. When we first stepped into the adoption agency we were told that the wait would be long - 18 months to two years, possibly longer. In our case, God had no such time frame. Even before we had finished our letter the social worker called and asked us to finish it quickly so that she could present it to a birth mom whom she had in mind. One week later we got another call. We had been chosen by a birth mom and she wanted to meet us in person.

Through our social worker we arranged to meet for lunch at the nearest Olive Garden. Our social worker would attend as well with the young woman who could potentially become our birth mom. We learned all the information about her before we even met. It was at this point that our vision of who our birth mom might be was turned upside down. We had expected to learn about a young high school or college-age girl who had found herself in a difficult situation. The woman we were about to meet was 26 years old and married. She and her husband were having difficulties and she subsequently chose to have an affair. Three affairs in fact, which meant three potential birth fathers. Her husband on learning of the pregnancy asked that she give the baby up for adoption as he did not want a "reminder" walking around in his home. The couple already had one child and were living on a small income. Their decision to give the baby up for adoption was a courageous one.

I remember being very nervous and praying a lot that morning. How do you prepare to meet a woman who could give you her child? Her child. The most precious gift she could give anyone. I felt like I was going on the biggest job interview of my life. What questions would she ask? What if I didn't look like a good mother type? What does a good mother look like, especially if she's not yet a mother? We prayed and asked God to be present in our meeting. If it wasn't to be, we felt that God would make it clear to us.

Our social worker and Abby met us there (this is not her real name: it has been changed to protect her). The woman before us was very nervous as well, visibly shaking and laughing nervously. She was about 5'10" with light brown hair, a fair complexion, and large glasses on her face. Abby was very pregnant but also very thin, almost anorexic looking. Her doctor had said that the baby boy was perfectly healthy despite her thin build but was taking all it needed from her. She shared that her husband was making sure that she was well taken care of and not forgetting to take her pre-natal vitamins each day. As the four of us talked, the conversation did not lull. Questions were answered, impressions given, God was there. Abby was a Christian as well and talked about the fact that she knew she had made a mistake but now wanted something good to come out of the situation. She and her husband were in counseling to try to put the pieces of their marriage back together. We left the lunch feeling like it had gone well. Our social worker whispered that she'd give us a call soon to let us know Abby's impression. The following morning we got the call we had been waiting for. "Get ready to be parents."

Abby wasn't due for another month so we decided to take a little vacation to Oregon to visit some close friends who had just had a new baby of their own. We went out and purchased our first cell phone so we could be contacted in case Abby went into early labor. It was a fun time as we were joyful about the fact that we would have a baby in our house very soon. Knowing that we had been chosen by a birth mom, we were still very cautious in sharing the news. Our families knew that we were in the midst of adopting a baby, but we didn't tell anyone that we had been chosen. We had heard too many stories about heartbroken couples who were days away from bringing a baby home only to have an adoption fall through. We chose not to make any big plans in anticipation of the baby who was soon to grace our home. Driving home from Oregon we chatted excitedly about the baby, what we needed to do to prepare the house, ourselves, and mostly about how our life was about to change in a big way. This was an interesting time. Most couples have 6 - 9 months to prepare for their first baby. We had walked into the adoption agency in January, here it was in mid June and our baby would be arriving any day. Aaron's parents had purchased a beautiful crib for us in hopes that we'd soon make them grandparents. We finally put it together and decorated the nursery in a Noah's Ark theme. We spent our last days without children feverishly painting the nursery, staying up until the wee hours of the morning, too excited to sleep and wanting to finish the baby's room. All the while in the back of our minds we knew that Abby could still change her mind. Until she signed the papers it was not a done deal.

The call came on a Thursday morning, June 24th, at 8am when I was at work. "Your son was born last night. 8 pounds, 13 ounces, 21" long. Strong and healthy. Abby is doing fine, she had a good delivery." As I hung up the phone, tears in my eyes, the office erupted around me. I was smothered with hugs and there wasn't a dry eye to be seen since all of my co-workers knew what had just happened. I quickly called Aaron. "You're a Daddy. Your son was born last night." My husband is rarely speechless but at this life-changing news, he was. At the time I was working at an orthopaedic office that was right across the street from St. Mary's Hospital, the very hospital that our new baby son was in. I so badly wanted to see him but couldn't per the arrangement we had made. We had decided that this would be Abby's time with the baby. We would have him the rest of our lives, she would have him for three days.

Even though our son had been born, we were very cautious. He wasn't ours yet. Not until we could hold him in our arms did we dare hold him in our hearts. Abby could still change her mind within those three days. We didn't even share the exciting news with our families. The next two nights were sleepless for us; we joked that God was preparing us to have a new baby in the house. We spent that Saturday at Target, getting bottles and formula, tiny little footed jammies and whatever last minute things we thought we'd need. Weeks before at a cute little baby clothing store in the mall we'd found an outfit for our son to wear home from the hospital. Blue and yellow plaid overalls with a baby blue shirt and a hat to match were chosen and given to the social worker. She made sure Abby would receive them to dress the baby in. When we first saw him, that's what he was wearing.

Sunday morning, June 27th, was Placement Day. We shared a quiet breakfast over coffee and cinnamon rolls, treasuring the moment. It felt strange. We were about to become parents and we were sitting in the dining room and not in a labor and delivery room. We knew our life would never be the same and yet we were very excited about the change that was just hours away. Aaron's father made a surprise visit to our house that morning, having no idea what was going on. Thankfully all the bottles and supplies had been neatly put away in our kitchen cabinets so there was no evidence that someone new was arriving at our house later that day. He knew we were getting ready to adopt so the crib and the stroller were not a giveaway. The giveaway should have been that we were about to burst with nervous energy and joy. For him it was just a regular visit and he left having no idea that he was about to be called Grandpa. We left our house just after noon with the car seat and a cozy blanket placed in the back seat, not really knowing if we'd bring a baby back with us.

We didn't chat much as we made the 20 minute drive to the park that was a block away from the agency. We were told to wait there until the papers had been signed. We were nervous and fearful that she would change her mind. The social worker had told us that Abby was doing well. She had spent the night before at home with her family while the baby spent the night at the social worker's home which was commonplace. Abby and her husband would arrive at the agency first where she'd sign the papers and then spend the last few moments with her baby. The thought of her grief in that moment broke my heart. Her world would be full of sadness, while ours would be full of joy because of the decision she would make that day. We prayed that God would be her Comforter. We were praying for her when the cell phone rang. She had signed the papers. "Come and meet your son."

It was a beautiful day and as we walked up the steps of the agency, I recalled the first time we had walked up those stairs only 6 months earlier. We were amazed at how God had crushed the expected time frame of two years and allowed us to have this wonderful baby in such a short time. As we walked in, Abby was sitting on the sofa with the baby while her husband Kent sat in a cozy chair by the window. He was a very sweet man and acknowledged us as we walked into the room. Before I laid eyes on my new baby boy, I hugged Abby first, seeing the tears in her eyes. She laid him in my arms and then we sat together on the sofa just taking him in. I told her how beautiful her baby was and thanked her for taking such good care of him. I thanked her for giving us this baby that was already filling our life with such joy.

As Aaron finished signing his paperwork, Abby got up to let him meet his son. His eyes immediately filled with tears as I handed him his first child. It was love at first sight for us. This beautiful boy was the most perfect baby we had ever seen. We sat together sharing the moment centered around our new son, knowing that God had planned it all along. Near the end of our time together we all stood up, joined hands and Aaron prayed. He thanked God first for Abby and Kent and their unselfish love for this baby. He thanked God for this little gift He'd placed in our lives. He prayed for wisdom and blessing upon our new family. By this time every person in the room was crying. Kent was sobbing in the background as we prayed, saying later that he knew how his wife's heart was breaking but that she was joyful as well to have found the perfect parents for her baby. It was a bittersweet moment as they left the agency with empty arms and our arms were finally full.

We named him Titus David Haslem.

Placement day with our new baby son.

CHAPTER 2

Early Days with Titus

As we drove home from the adoption agency, we were as close to heaven on earth as two people can get. It was instant parenthood. All of a sudden there was a carseat in the back of *our* car with *our* baby in it! We had no adjustment time in the hospital, no feeding help from kind nurses, but also no stitches or pain medication. When we showed up at our home, our garage featured a gigantic sign: "It's a Boy" surrounded by assorted shades of blue balloons. Some sweet friends of ours had been certain that we would be bringing home a baby boy that day. A flurry of phone calls ensued. First we called Aaron's parents in Montana, the grandfather that asked me on our wedding day, "When am I going to be called Grandpa?" Titus was their first grandchild. They thought Aaron was joking as he shared the news, then Titus quietly cooed. Silence was what we got, then disbelief, then the sounds of crying. There was no Skype in 1999 and we didn't have instant digital photos or Facebook to share our little miracle. We continued the phone calls to all of my family and the rest of Aaron's. The reactions were priceless. Stunned silence, disbelief and happiness. It was great fun to have Aaron's father show up once again that day. Tears rolled down his face as he held his first grandson. Titus was showered with love as packages and cards for him were a daily occurrence for the first month. So many people had been praying for the arrival of this little boy long before he was a thought, and they all delightedly welcomed him into the world.

The first weeks and months of having a new baby in our home were pure bliss. Just like any other new parents, we were tired, but we savored the moments of caring for the baby we had so longed for. Titus was a captivating baby with a bit of sandy blonde hair and those mesmerizing blue eyes. Even as a newborn he had almost no fat on his body and a very long torso. He was a peaceful, contented baby and slept through the night at 7 weeks thanks to the tips we learned in our new favorite book, *BabyWise*. I would spend hours just cuddling him in the rocking chair. One afternoon Aaron came home from work to find dirty dishes piled in the sink and me in the rocking chair with Titus, in the same position I was in when he had left that morning.

"What have you been doing all day?" he asked, his voice a bit biting.

"I've been bonding with YOUR son!"

I did so love holding my new son, and I felt was important to make up for the 9 months that he didn't spend within my body. A good friend of ours who happened to be a massage therapist taught us how to do baby massage. We would do massage from head to toe after his bath each night using a special lavender scented lotion. He loved the routine of it all and we felt that he slept much better because of it.

When he was 6 months old, we dedicated Titus to The Lord at a church ceremony. It was a sweet day and also the day that Titus received one of his most treasured possessions, Blue Bunny. "Blue," as he is affectionately known, was about as big as Titus at the time with soft baby blue fur and long ears. Most days Blue was tenderly dragged around the house and his ears were sucked, turning brown from all the loving. I would have to wash him at night after Titus had fallen asleep. One time, though, Titus put Blue in the potty and defiantly refused to take him out. Over the years, Blue has been with Titus as a constant in the chaos. He's been on every long car trip and plane ride we've ever taken. I don't think there's ever been a night that Blue hasn't been where Titus slept. As long as Blue was with us, Titus felt safe.

Titus and Blue Bunny.

Even before Aaron and I married we had decided that we didn't want our children raised by anyone else but us. Our relationship began at a church where we both served on staff in the children's ministry department. Through the years, we had taught children of all ages and admired those families who were committed to one or both parents staying home with the children. With this unique insight we made a commitment to work hard enough that one of us could always be home with our children. In honor of this commitment, after 3 months of maternity leave I went back to work at the clinic part time, working early morning hours. Aaron would meet me in the parking lot with Titus and we would swap. Aaron would spend the mornings with Titus, hand him off to me, go on to his classes at the University, then work his 6 - 8 hours as a forklift driver, not to return until almost midnight. After returning home he would study until Titus's 2 am feeding. Since we saw each other for so few minutes during the day, we used to write messages to each other on the bathroom mirror using a dry erase marker. It was a crazy schedule but it worked for us and Titus. The experience would serve him well later, as he learned to adjust to different schedules every semester. This way of life continued until Aaron graduated two years later.

Another aspect of our crazy schedule would come to serve Titus quite well. For a brief time, Titus was able to come to work with me for half hour increments. Being the handsome baby that he was, my co-workers just couldn't resist grabbing him out of his car seat and taking him on little walks during their breaks. Titus was a very social baby, due in part to the many times he was passed around. One memorable moment in the office came when I was chatting with some of the gals in a department on my floor.

One of them asked me, "So, does Titus look like his real mother?" I was taken aback but responded, "I am his real mother." She responded with a giggle, "Oh, you know what I mean."

Yes, I knew what she meant, but it's always been important to us to not make an adopted child somehow less than a biological child. I remember one instance of a friend making reference to an adopted child as a "stray." Adoption is not for everyone, for sure, but we don't see any difference: he is our child, hand picked by God. To answer the question, Titus happens to look a lot like me and my dad. An old framed photograph hung on our wall, a large black and white photo that had been colorized. It shows a blonde 2-year-old in baby blue overalls and a bright smile. The photo is of my dad back in the 1930's.

My dad was visiting our home one day and commented, "That's a great one of Titus. It's so unusual."

"Dad... that's a picture of you," I said.

"Well, isn't that something," he replied as tears filled his eyes.

Beyond that, there are the birthmarks. I'm sure it was an ordinary day as a busy mom when I realized that Titus and I have the same birthmarks. I have a birthmark on my right shoulder and a birthmark on my left jaw. Titus also has one on his right shoulder and one on his left jaw. God knew the future of my little son. He knew the challenges that would lie ahead. With those birthmarks, He was showing me in a very visual way, "See? I hand-picked this child for you. I didn't make a mistake. You are the best mother for this little boy." I have thought of those birthmarks along with the reassuring promise many times over the years.

Titus was an exceptionally happy baby.

Titus's first year of life was essentially normal. We fell in love with the little guy more each day and we knew he was brilliant. He hit all the milestones at the regular times. Eating and sleeping were never a problem; he rolled over, crawled and walked right on schedule. It was at this age that he discovered computers. He would sit on Dad's lap as he studied and just watch. He loved anything to do with computers. The sight of Dad's laptop on the floor is what coaxed him into crawling.

We had started teaching Titus baby sign language at about 9 months of age. So when he wasn't talking much at 12 months, we weren't too concerned. We just figured that since he was so good at signing what he wanted, he didn't need to to use words. He knew the signs for "eat," "drink," "all done," "more," "please," and "thank you." This pattern continued through the 18-month mark. At this time, he still had a very small vocabulary. He said all the usual first words: "Momma," "Da-da," "ju" (juice), "bye-bye," and, of course, "no," his favorite word.

He was always very social -- smiling and giggly; he loved being around people and they adored him. I remember thinking that he should have more words by now, because we read to him constantly, played music and talked to him all the time. At his 18-month check up I shared my concern with his pediatrician. "He's developing within the normal parameters for a baby his age," the doctor told me; I was "a first time mom" and shouldn't be "overly concerned." I'd had much experience with children and babies in previous years and still felt he should be talking more. Despite this, I trusted the knowledge and wisdom of the young pediatrician and assumed he knew more than I did.

Titus at 18 months old.

When a doctor has told you that your chances of having a baby are "one in a million," and you've been through infertility, the last thing on your mind is birth control. Consequently, the day before Titus turned 1 year old we found out that I was 7 weeks pregnant. A friend had convinced me to take a pregnancy test, though I thought I'd taken enough of those. It was positive. Still in denial, I left Titus with my friend and made an appointment for that day and was able to get an ultrasound done right away. Tears filled my eyes as I heard the whoosh, whoosh, whoosh of my baby's heartbeat. The doctor said everything looked great and baby was strong and healthy. My hands shook as I took the little ultrasound pictures to the frame department of a local store. I framed a precious little photo and drove to Aaron's work. I had him paged and as he walked into the room his face was anxious.

"What's wrong? Is Titus okay?" I just handed him the photo. . . he looked at it, looked at me, and at the photo again in disbelief.

"You're going to be a daddy again."

We were in shock for a couple of weeks. Imagine the stares we got at the adoption reunion, held in September for all the couples who had adopted throughout that year. It was quite awkward and we almost didn't attend knowing it might be difficult for other couples. Some people could barely look at us, let alone speak to us. Others were warm and genuine and truly excited for us. In October of 1999, when we finalized the adoption, I was 7 months pregnant. I'm quite sure the judge hadn't had many cases such as ours. Our social worker greeted us there, delighted for us, being blessed with not only Titus but another little someone. God's plan was so amazing. He needed Titus to be in our home and we knew it. When we share the story, people tend to say things like "Well, I've heard that happens a lot," or "See, all you needed to do was relax." We are quick to give the glory to God in our response, "God closed my womb until Titus was in our home. He knew we needed each other." We never had infertility issues again--in fact quite the opposite has happened. God does have a sense of humor and has enjoyed blessing our family. We consider each one of our children to be a miracle.

Our son Noah was born at the end of January, weighing almost 8 pounds. He brought much joy to our home; in fact, the most difficult part of having Noah in our life has been his delivery. From day one he has been a tenderhearted soul with wisdom far beyond his years. Titus seemed excited about the new baby in the house. He was a busy toddler and was mostly self entertained but he did love to help me with the new baby. He wasn't at all jealous or rough with the baby, but like any parents, we watched their interactions carefully. Noah was a chubby, happy little man who loved his older brother from the very beginning. They would watch each other in wonder during the day. I could set Noah in the middle of the floor in his bouncy seat and he would just watch Titus go around and around the room. As Noah grew into toddlerhood I watched carefully as he reached all the milestones. I was especially thankful that his language skills exploded about the time he started walking.

In the spring of that year, Aaron's brother was married in North Carolina. We made the trek with our almost 2-year-old and our 4-month-old by plane across the country to attend the big event. Titus did well on our adventure until about day 3. Day 3 for him has historically been the breaking point, the day he's done holding himself together in the midst of change and chaos. Unfortunately Aaron missed most of the wedding because Titus was having one of his first meltdowns in the car. At this point a meltdown consisted of anxiety, defiance and crying, followed by inconsolable screaming until he finally fell asleep This is one of the few times we spent with Aaron's family and I wondered what impression we left on everyone. Titus was a delightful little boy but he definitely had some issues that must have concerned our family, yet they were too polite or too passive to say anything. I suppose it helped that Noah was a chubby-cheeked smiling baby who was happily passed around. Over the years we have missed many events, usually when we're traveling and it's all become too much for Titus. It's difficult to explain to people why we didn't make it, so we usually give some excuse instead of explaining the real reason.

In June, Aaron graduated from The University of Nevada - Reno after 7 years of hard work for both of us. He took his first engineering job in Carson City, which allowed me to quit my job at the Orthopaedic clinic and stay home full time. I was delighted: all I ever really wanted as a career was to be a mommy. Our dream at the time was to move to Oregon where we had visited years before. Oregon reminded us of the beauty of Montana and, at that time, had the jobs that Montana didn't. A former co-worker of mine had moved there with her husband, who also happened to be an engineer, accepting a job on the Oregon Coast.

As she left I asked her to let us know if any engineering jobs came up. In February of 2002, we got a call for a job interview and took a quick trip to Oregon, leaving the boys with friends and family.

Just a couple of months before, I'd had some familiar clues and consequently took another pregnancy test. Aaron took one look at the plus sign on the stick and looked at me.

"Are you sure? These things can be wrong, right?" he said, pointing at the stick.

"I'm pretty sure I'm pregnant. I've had all the other familiar signs," I said, smiling.

Aaron had endured me taking so many pregnancy tests over the years, I don't suppose I blame him for not believing me until he saw an actual ultrasound of baby #3. Of course we hadn't used birth control, thinking that Noah was our "one in a million" baby. Looking back, I am so glad that we were pregnant before Titus was diagnosed. The news might have caused us to reconsider other children, and we would have missed out on raising an absolutely amazing daughter.

Looking back, we see some red flags in addition to his lack of words. As a toddler, Titus would never gesture for things he wanted. He was mostly independent in that regard: if he needed something he would attempt to get it himself or wait until we offered it to him. At the time, we were amazed at how content he was. He could play by himself for long periods of time and watch half-hour videos from his swing. Whenever he got a new truck or any other toy with wheels, he would not play with it in the appropriate way. There were no boy noises and he would immediately turn the toy over and spin the wheels around and around. Instead of playing with little cars, he would line them all up in a long row. If we moved one he would see and take it and put it back in his correct order. At his 2-year check up I again voiced my concerns about his lack of language. The pediatrician again reassured me that though his verbal capacity was "a little behind," he was still developing fine. He said that I was "an overprotective first-time mom" and that I needed to "relax and not worry."

Right around the 2 ½ year milestone, Titus had stopped saying "bye-bye." We thought maybe it was part of his adjustment to having baby Noah around. One morning soon after, I decided to take Titus and Noah to a preschool story time at the local library. Titus was a bit restless as he sat with the other preschoolers while I sat in the back feeding Noah. But when the teacher started leading the kids in a song, Titus started screaming. This wasn't just fussing: this was high-pitched, uncontrollable, clawing me in an "I want out of here now!" way. I had never seen him act like that. I grabbed him up in one arm and Noah in the other and left the library right away. Titus was still screaming and didn't calm down until we walked through our front door. I was really concerned. I called the pediatrician later that day and scheduled an appointment. I thought perhaps he had an ear infection and the singing may have caused his ears to hurt. In the back of my mind was the possibility that something more serious was wrong.

Later that week, I took him in for his 2 ½ year check up. There was no sign of ear infection. As the pediatrician finished the exam I mustered up my courage.

"Titus still only has a few words. He has even stopped using a few of them. He stopped saying bye-bye. There is something wrong with my son. I need you to refer me to a speech therapist or someone who can help with his language." My voice was shaking. "I am not being overprotective. Please give me a referral to someone or I will find a doctor who will."

The doctor shrugged his shoulders as he handed me a slip of paper with a number on it. *Special Children's Clinic*.

Two weeks later we visited the Special Children's Clinic. We had our first appointment in mid-February, which consisted of medical history forms, parent questionnaires, a hearing test, a general physical, and a one-hour observation of Titus. By the end of our time that day, they'd concluded that Titus had "language and social skills deficits that were significant enough to warrant further testing." An appointment was scheduled for two weeks later to "rule out autism." While we waited, I decided to do some of my own research on autism. This was the first of many research sessions we have done on behalf of our beloved son over the years. I learned that a group of professionals had to agree on a diagnosis of autism. One day that week, I decided to have a conversation with my close friend Margie. She had a son with autism who was 4 at the time and I knew in my heart I needed to call her but I was hesitant. We had seen Margie and her family just 3 months before while in Montana for the holidays. When I spoke to her on the phone that day she cried as she told me that she noticed some familiar characteristics in Titus that she had seen in her own son. "I wish I would have said something ... and I don't know why I didn't." As I hung up the phone, I knew already that my son had autism. It was a crushing feeling. My heart sank and tears ran down my cheeks as I looked at my happy, innocent little boy running towards me. I knew from that day on things would never be "normal" for him or our family. Over the years I've come to cherish that fact because normal is so overrated. Looking back, this was the day that I first grieved the loss of a normal life for my son. The conversation with my friend Margie was a way of The Lord softening the blow of what was coming.

The speech pathologist showed up at our door two weeks later with clipboard in hand. Titus greeted her at the door with a big smile and excitedly helped her bring in a bag. They sat together on the floor as she brought out several manipulatives and puzzles for Titus to work with. She conducted two different assessments as they played. He was content and happy throughout the session and even shared Blue Bunny and some crackers with her.

As she left she said, "He is a delightful little boy and did very well today. I don't think he has autism."

The research I had done resonated in my head as I said, "Isn't an evaluation of this nature done as a group?"

She looked at me and sighed heavily, "Well ... we are just so busy at the clinic. There just isn't time and we are shorthanded at the moment. That's really not possible."

"Honestly," I said, "I don't care if you're short handed. This is my son. You are a very nice person and this is nothing personal but I can't base the rest of my son's life on just your opinion. This could affect the rest of his life."

I am generally a very shy person, but at this moment the mama bear inside me came out, reassuring me that the bond between Titus and I was real -- adopted or not. It surprised me how it rose to the surface and I couldn't hold it in. An appointment was scheduled a few days later.

On that morning in March, five professionals in the room observed Titus: a speech-language pathologist, a social worker, an occupational therapist, a child psychologist, and a pediatrician, plus our little family. Noah was just walking and Ciciley was in my tummy. Aaron and I both knew before we walked through the doors what the result would be. We watched quietly in the corner of a large playroom as the group of five played with Titus and observed his behavior. An hour later we all sat in a circle and talked about their results. The findings of the report stated that he was "mild to severely delayed in his communication and self-help skills. Diagnosis: Autism Spectrum Disorder."

As gently as he could, the speech-language specialist stated the facts. "Your son is in the mid-range of the autism spectrum. His social skills are on the higher end and that is his strength. His communication however is on the low end and that will be where he will struggle. Specialized early intervention would be beneficial. You'll need to contact the school district that you'll be moving into in Oregon."

They proceeded to show us the charts and numbers and explain what an IEP (Individual Education Plan) was. For me the words were a blur and I just wanted to hug my little boy. He was still Titus. He was still our precious son. It was the beginning of a long journey and all we had was a candle in the dark unknown of it all. We did know that God wasn't surprised by the news. God reminded me that He doesn't make mistakes. God reminded me that I was hand-chosen to be his Mommy. Not on that day or any other day has there ever been an ounce of regret that Titus was our son. A blanket of Peace covered our little family that day. Even though it was difficult to hear the official diagnosis, we knew that Our God had a reason for it all and we prayed that day that He would be glorified in the long road ahead.

Soon after we got the official diagnosis, I called Titus' pediatrician back and left a message with his nurse. "Just let him know that Titus was diagnosed with autism." I was angry at his lack of concern. I've often wondered what his reaction was. Thankfully, these days pediatricians are much more in tune to the early symptoms of autism. Personally, I don't believe that autism is being diagnosed more because of this awareness, but because there are actually more cases now than ever before. When Titus was born, about 1 in 150 kids was diagnosed with autism. Today, 15 years later, about 1 in 68 kids is thus diagnosed. I don't hold anything against our pediatrician; it probably wouldn't have made much of a difference in my son's life if he'd been diagnosed 6 months earlier. I do hope that the pediatrician has learned to listen to "first-time moms" and added certain tests in his exams that would find autism, or any sort of developmental delay, early on.

I also hope that research into the causes of autism continues to progress. Long before Andrew Wakefield and Jenny McCarthy made headlines, we had our concerns about vaccinations. In fact, Aaron did a research paper on the safety of vaccinations right about the time Titus was about 6 months old. Though we did have a conversation in which Aaron expressed he thought we should wait on the vaccinations, I thought we should listen to our pediatrician and the medical community as a whole and vaccinate him according to all the schedules, which we did. One of my first remarks to Aaron after we found out our son had autism, was "Please, please don't blame me." He never did blame me, of course, but after that we have chosen not to vaccinate our other children in the same way. We waited until they were all older than two, being very cautious along the way. I am not saying that a vaccine caused my son's autism, but it may have somehow triggered it. As of the writing of this book, there is no known cause of autism. More research into causes and treatments is badly needed.

Two weeks later we packed up our family and moved to Oregon.

Chapter 3

Missing at Church

Packing with two busy toddlers when I was 7 months pregnant was an adventure in itself. We did most of the packing at night while the boys were asleep. We loaded up the biggest moving truck we could find and excitedly headed to Oregon. On moving day we left five hours behind schedule, Aaron driving the truck and I with my blossoming tummy driving the car with the boys in the back. We got about two miles down the road when a tire blew on the moving truck, right in the middle of "the spaghetti bowl," as it's known in Reno, Nevada. It's an awful mess of winding concrete where two major interstates intersect. Thankfully we had walkie talkies so we could communicate with each other. It took about three hours for the repair truck to find us in the beginning of rush hour traffic. I somehow found a way to entertain Titus and Noah in the back seat with Veggietales music, numerous renditions of *Wheels on The Bus*, and the snacks that were supposed to last for 12 hours. Of course at that time we didn't have a convenient little invention like a DVD player in the car. Four hours after the tire had blown, we were on our way. Six hours later we were completely exhausted and found a hotel in the wee hours of the morning. It was then that Noah, now wide awake, decided he wanted to play. It was an auspicious beginning to our time spent in Oregon.

We arrived in Oregon on a wet and stormy afternoon. It hadn't rained for over a week before we arrived, but it started raining as we neared the coastal town of Tillamook, and it rained for 7 more days without stopping. Aaron's new co-workers warmly welcomed us at our new rental house and helped us empty all our belongings. That first week we met the people at the specialized preschool that Titus would be attending in the fall. Everyone we encountered that day was very friendly and very aware of the fact that everything they said, every term was new to our vocabulary. We met his speech therapist, an autism specialist, an occupational therapist, and his delightful young preschool teacher. She made an impression on us when she mentioned that her sister was autistic and she had a real love for children with autism. Later that week the autism specialist visited our home as they needed to make their own diagnosis. At the time, it was puzzling since the paperwork we already had in hand stated his diagnosis, but we found that each new school district is obligated to do this to get funding for each individual with special needs in their district. We never saw these visits as invasive or unnecessary. We took each new event as easily as we could, learning along the way that most people who are in special education really do care about your children and want the best for them. Some of the problems within special education ultimately come down to the budget and the people at the top of the ladder who are not face-to-face with your child every day. Another frustrating aspect is that laws involving special education are always changing; what was available last year may not be available this year.

We spent our first months in Oregon adjusting to our new "normal" as well as getting ready for our baby girl to arrive. It was a grand time of discovery for our Titus. One morning I happened to find him on the floor next to a box of Aaron's old engineering textbooks that were in the corner of boxes yet to be unpacked. He had found one in particular and had it turned to the page on technical writing examples: actual letters and how to write them. He still barely spoke 15 words so I had never even attempted working with him on his letters, but I thought I'd sit for a moment and see what I could teach him.

I was amazed that as I pointed to the letter "A," he said "A."

"Okay," I thought, "lucky guess."

"B," "C," "D," he continued as I pointed.

"Alright... let's try a different line and out of order," I thought to myself.

"M," "X," "F," he continued.

I cried tears of joy right there as we sat with the book and he knew every single letter. He could barely speak, yet he knew all his letters without me lifting a finger. It was then that I remembered that earlier in the week he'd been watching *Wheel of Fortune* on the TV as I made dinner. He had learned all his letters from a game show in a matter of days. That was when we discovered what an awesome visual learner he was.

One memorable afternoon later that summer I developed an advanced radar system. Every mom has a "radar." It shows up the minute that little one comes into your life. I have regular mom radar for my neurotypical children, but with Titus I discovered that I needed something more. Noah was napping and Titus was watching a favorite Veggietales movie in the front room. I decided to take care of a few piles of laundry and do some vacuuming upstairs. After a few minutes the phone rang. I shut off the vacuum and picked up the phone.

"Hi, it's Heidi, I just wanted to let you know that Titus is fine."

Heidi was our sweet neighbor who had a new baby of her own.

"Ah... yes... he is fine." I was confused. "He's just watching a movie downstairs."

"Umm... no. He's here at my house playing with toys. He just walked in a couple of minutes ago. He's so cute. He just walked right in and made himself at home."

"Oh my goodness. I'm so sorry. I'll be right over to get him."

My smart little son had waited until I started vacuuming then he unlocked and opened up the screen door and wandered over to the neighbor's house, whom we had visited once. I quickly walked over and gathered my son and attempted to explain to him that he had to ask Mommy before we visit our friends. I tried to be calm and not overreact in front of him. But I was worried. He could have wandered into the pond just below our house or up to the street at the end of our driveway. And thankfully it was a neighbor we could trust. It was quite nerve wracking to me to have an autistic son who liked to wander and was oblivious to danger. I've had to keep an extra close eye on him ever since.

Our baby girl, Ciciley Anna, arrived in late July: a petite 6 pounds, 7 ounces and 18 inches long. She had the puffiest dark hair that we'd ever seen on a baby and she was so irresistible that the nurses would fight over who got to hold her. Dad brought the boys over to meet their little sister the next day. Titus came and gave his new baby sister a little kiss on the cheek and then was off to play with the balloons that decorated the room. When we came home later that week I was a very busy mama with three in diapers. Titus was just not getting the whole potty training idea and Noah was just 18 months old at the time, far from even starting. Titus reacted well to his new baby sister, but he wasn't as aware of her as he had been of Noah when Noah was a baby. He was busy learning so many new things: when he did play with his sister I would grab a camera, since it happened so rarely. For a few months afterward I went through post-partum depression, and my food allergies flared up, due in part to the stress of what was on my plate. A lot had happened in the past 6 months: the diagnosis, a huge move, and a new baby. Most days were exhausting and I would try to schedule naps so that everyone, including me, could take a rest.

Titus playing with baby Ciciley.

One particular day was especially difficult as we headed out to the local library. It was commonplace in our household then, and now, to watch time very carefully so as not to upset the delicate balance of Titus' tendency to rely on time. We had just gotten out of the car and headed up the steps. The sign above the door said *OPEN,* but when his eager little hand reached for the handle, it did not turn. I knew it was coming: immediate frustration. Titus started screaming as loud as he could. Screaming because the library was supposed to open at 10 a.m. It was two minutes past ten. We had waited in the car until 10:01, just to make sure a situation like this would not occur.

I tried my best to calm him.

"I know it's 10:02. Yes, I know the door is locked. The person inside is late. I'm so sorry, Titus. I know you are upset."

The screaming just got louder and more high-pitched. Titus, still only speaking a handful of words, could not communicate his emotions verbally. Screaming was his only way of expressing his frustration. Noah, unfazed by the screams, was checking out the cool bugs on the sidewalk. Ciciley in the car seat, however, was startled awake and began to cry. Just then, a woman walked up behind us and stood for a minute, obviously alarmed by the screaming scene.

I spoke as kindly to her as I could over the screams. "I'm sorry about this. The library was supposed to open four minutes ago and my son just doesn't understand. He has autism."

"Labels just give kids an excuse to misbehave," she said coolly.

"Labels just give kids an excuse to misbehave." The words sank to my very soul. Did she really say that about my precious son? There I stood, speechless on the steps of the little library. In shock, all I could do was let my jaw drop open and hold back the tears. A minute later the door to the library opened and the 50-something woman pushed in front of our foursome to get to her important library business, shaking her head impatiently. The screaming stopped as soon as we entered and my boys went to the beloved children's section while I found a spot to get comfy and feed my littlest one. We spent a few quiet minutes in that place but my mind was racing.

I continued to stifle the tears until I had put all of my children back into the car and headed to Aaron's workplace. I couldn't go home just yet. I needed to share my heart with my husband, who worked only ten minutes away. As soon as I turned the key in the ignition, I could hold back no longer and tears streamed down my cheeks.

"Is Mommy okay?" came a sweet little voice from the back seat.

"Yes Noah, Mommy is okay. Sometimes Mommies cry too."

So many thoughts rumbled around in my head and my heart. This woman had no idea what life was like at my house. From her appearance, I supposed that her children were grown and gone and blissfully "normal." To this day I'm sure she has no idea what a scar she left on my heart that morning.

I arrived at Aaron's office, sobbing as the boys made their rounds to all the friendly people with whom he worked. I told him all about it and of course he came up with several comebacks on the spot, a talent I've often envied. When I had calmed down and was able to drive home, God gently reminded me of the birthmarks. That day was one of a handful of days when ignorant people have come into our lives for a split second. It was the day I realized that our other children would be deeply impacted by their brother, and the day that I realized that Noah had taken over the role of older brother. Up until this time we really hadn't expected it, but had prayed that he would never be embarrassed or sorry that his brother was different. Since that day, Noah has taken the role with grace, never complaining or expressing embarrassment. This is one of those areas where we as parents have to pray for our children and trust God to develop character in them through the disability of their brother.

In August of that summer, Aaron took a road trip with Titus back down to Reno. Per our adoption agreement, Abby was entitled to two visits before Titus turned 3 years old. The first visit was a play date at a local park the previous summer. It was a very nice visit and Abby had brought some little gifts to show her affection for Titus. She seemed happy to see all of us and she admired Titus and attempted to give him hugs. Of course he knew nothing about her or who she was; we just explained that this is Mommy and Daddy's friend. For this final visit, they all met at a local McDonalds. Abby came with Kent and their 5 year old son. As they were eating, the 5 year old spilled ketchup on the table and Abby became very upset, yelling at her young son, fearful that he would get a stain on his shirt. A few moments later, Abby began expressing some concerns about Titus. "How come he's not potty trained yet? He really should be potty trained by now." "Why isn't he talking more?" It was during this time that Aaron gently explained to Abby that Titus had autism. She seemed very confused about it all and proceeded to ask again, "Why isn't he potty trained?" After awhile she expressed her disappointment in the fact that Aaron hadn't brought me and the new baby girl with him. She was really looking forward to seeing the baby. Afterward, Aaron thought she seemed more concerned about why the baby wasn't there than about Titus' diagnosis. The whole visit just confirmed the fact that Titus belonged in our family. We knew that Abby would have been unable to deal with his disability. About a year later we received a call from our social worker. Abby had become pregnant again and wanted to give the baby up for adoption. "Would we like to adopt again?" We took a day to seriously think about it but decided we already had our hands quite full with the three we had. I'm sure that the baby ended up in another wonderful family. We haven't heard from Abby or our adoption agency since that time.

Titus started preschool that September and his first day was a memorable one. He was thrilled to be able to ride the bus. He and I watched out the window for the little yellow bus to arrive and he jumped up and down as it pulled up to the house. I walked him on to the bus and buckled him in. He seemed such a tiny guy on that first day, strapped into a booster seat with Blue and his little red Dr. Seuss backpack. He looked at me as if to say, "Hurry up Mom, I got somewhere to go." I waved and waved at him as the bus drove away and he stared out the window with his bright blue eyes. As the bus disappeared around a turn, I burst into tears. Sending my precious three year old away on a bus to specialized preschool was a moment I hadn't quite imagined. I called Aaron at work and all I could do was cry. Noah was always there watching me with his big green eyes and tender soul. Several times that day he would just come and sit by my side. He has been a source of comfort throughout the years for reasons I can't really explain other than to say he was there at every early moment of grief, even when he was far from understanding it all.

Soon after Titus started preschool, I gave my own mother a call. She was eager to know how all "her babies" were doing. I gave her the scoop on her beautiful new granddaughter and how Noah was pretending to read already. I told her all about Titus' preschool and what he was doing.

"He's really doing great, Mom. He loves riding the bus and he's learned all his letters and is working on saying his numbers."

"Does he have lots of new friends in the classroom?"

"Um… well… there are about 5 other kids in the classroom with him. He doesn't really make friends yet," I said. "All of the kids in his classroom have a disability of some kind. They really try to work with the children on a one-to-one basis."

"Well, I think that's just wonderful. He'll have such an appreciation for 'those people' when he grows up," she said knowingly.

I was quiet for a minute. "Um… Mom. He *is* one of "those people."

Silence. My mom loves to chat on the phone but those words went right to her heart.

"I guess I didn't realize how serious it is. Is this something he will grow out of?" she asked nervously.

"Well, Mom, autism is a life-long disability. There is no cure. He won't grow out of it but hopefully he'll learn how to function in the world. We are doing everything we can to help him, the special preschool is just the beginning."

She quickly changed the subject to her favorite topic of gardening.

Autism doesn't just affect our son. It affects us, our children, our parents, our siblings, and our friends. When Titus was first diagnosed, we told everyone in our family. We never hid the diagnosis or tried to minimize it. We have on occasion not told them about things that would have unnecessarily upset them when there was no way they could have helped. Since a year after we were married, we have lived states away from our families, not only by choice but because we needed a good salary to support our commitment to living on one income, something we couldn't find close to family. For the most part, we don't see them more than once a year. But because of the distance our family doesn't really know what our life is like. Some relationships started out strong and for unknown reasons have weakened over the years. God has been faithful to us in this area; when there have been no grandparents around for special occasions, He has filled the gap with dear friends who happen to be the grandparent type and have given our children the love and support they desire. Other relationships have gotten even stronger and more supportive through the struggles that we face and we enjoy visits from those loved ones. There are also relationships that were very distant that have grown surprisingly close and connected.

Titus's first year of specialized preschool provided such a solid foundation. The focus was on Titus learning several things. Typical preschool skills such as letters, numbers, and colors were taught but he also learned social skills: how to play with others, how to pretend, and how to initiate play. Swimming played a vital role in his social learning. He loves to swim and the staff took full advantage of that by planning specific social games into that "play" time. He also worked on self care skills such as potty training, hand washing, and dressing himself. An important goal of his first year of preschool was to learn 25 new words. One way his vocabulary was built was by using the PECS system -- Picture Exchange Communication System. PECS was really helpful in that Titus would choose a picture of something he wanted and hand it to the person. Then he would learn the new word via a visual picture card and the word. We used this system at home as well. For years afterward he used a PECS visual schedule at school. All these skills may seem simple, but for Titus and many kids on the spectrum it takes hours of work and loads of patience to teach even the simple things. Early intervention is so important. It's really the foundation for how they will function the rest of their life. The earlier the specialized attention begins, the better it is for the child since the brain is still pliable. Since day one, Titus has had speech therapy as well as occupational therapy.

At the end of that first year of preschool we took part in the Spring IEP meeting to plan for the following year. As we were sitting there chatting, someone stated, "We are so impressed by your involvement as parents."

"Really ? Why is that?" Aaron said.

"You would be surprised by the number of parents who don't even attend these meetings."

"Why wouldn't we? We want to be as involved and helpful as we can in his education and support you all as much as we can." Families have many reasons for not attending meetings regarding their children. From our perspective, we've always made the utmost effort to be there, to be present. This is vitally important for us. We have been *entrusted* with our children. We didn't make them, and they are not ours to do with what we please. They are not for us to get to 18 so we can let them loose on the world. They are not a burden, but His creation that we have been trusted with to raise and care for.

Titus at 5 years old.

That summer, we wanted to provide Titus with an activity that was fun as well as therapeutic. His occupational therapist told us about a special program in the area that used horses to help kids with disabilities. The program was called BEAT - Bradley Equine Assisted Therapy. The program helps kids in the psychological areas of self-confidence, patience, risk-taking, responsibility, and teamwork, just to name a few. It also helps with physical aspects such as muscle tone and strength, fine and gross motor skills, and balance. Titus had an amazingly patient trainer and a very special horse named Butterscotch. He loved riding once a week and getting to know how to take care of a horse. His self confidence got a boost as he learned how to control a large animal. He had a lesson every week for about a year.

Another important task we tackled that summer was Titus' health. We attended an autism conference early in the summer and had the privilege of meeting a Naturopathic doctor who specialized in the treatment of autism. He had a lot of information that was unfamiliar to us, so we decided to make an appointment for later that month. Some of the health issues that concerned us were the number of yeast infections Titus had been treated for; the bruises on his shins, which we couldn't figure out how he was getting; and the nutritional content of his diet (Titus was a very picky eater and would only eat a few favorite foods). Our first appointment lasted an hour and a half, and was more thorough than any appointment we'd ever had with a doctor. Dr. Dramov was very kind and asked us questions about Titus and his health since his birth. Then he examined Titus from head to toe. He suggested several things we might do to help our son. We had testing done to measure the levels of heavy metals in his system and we chose to take gluten and casein out of his diet. Gluten is essentially found in wheat products and casein is a milk protein.

While the diet is not beneficial for every child, we saw some significant changes. Two weeks after his diet change, one evening at bedtime he hopped into his bed, hitting his shins on the metal bedframe,

"Ahhhhggghhh..." he groaned as he held his leg. This is where the bruises had come from, but it wasn't until that night that he was actually feeling the pain. That night we wrapped the bed frame with padding, and the bruises disappeared soon after.

Another unforgettable event happened a couple of days later. We were on a family excursion through our local Target store walking into the toy section.

"Hello Mr. Bear. How are you?" said a little voice behind me. At first I didn't catch it.

"What did you say, Noah?" I asked, assuming he had spoken. As I turned around and saw Noah a few feet away and Titus right behind me, I knelt down and said, "What did you say, Titus?" peering into those soft blue eyes.

"Hello Mr. Bear. How are you?" he said with a bright smile. Aaron and I looked at each other in amazement.

He had just spoken his *first sentence* right there in the middle of Target, and right there in the middle of Target we had a little celebration. Once again tears of joy filled my eyes as I gave my son a little hug.

In the fall, Titus started his second year of specialized preschool. He continued to work on many of the same goals as the previous year. He had some issues with being aggressive towards other students, but for the most part he was trying to initiate play since he didn't act in anger. It was during this time that he began to sneak food that wasn't his: a tiny chocolate candy, or a bite of cookie, whatever he could get his little hands on. Titus was becoming a sneaky little guy in a lot of areas. One evening at a church function he gave us a very big scare. We took the kids to church for our "married couples" meeting that met once every two weeks. There was childcare for our three little ones, so we took advantage of the wonderful fellowship and the free night out. About 20 minutes into our couples meeting, a woman approached our table and whispered into my ear, "We can't find your son Titus." Aaron and I quickly got to our feet and quietly walked out into the hallway.

"I don't know what happened! All the children were in the gym playing, and all of a sudden Titus was gone," said the woman with a worried tone.

Panic struck and I immediately started praying: "Lord help us find him."

We walked into the gym and Rachael, his special helper, ran over to us with a panicked look on her face. "I was watching him so closely. He waited until I looked away and out the door he went... over there by the drinking fountain." Tears filled her eyes as she pointed across the large gym to a metal door with a red EXIT sign above it. Titus had gotten direct access to the parking lot and the very busy street adjoining it. We hurried out the door to start the search, our concern heightened by the fact that darkness had just fallen. There must have been 10 volunteers looking for our son on the campus of the large church. We checked all around the main building, in bushes, in between the cars, all along the perimeter. I thought I should check our car in particular just in case he had found it. As I reached the car I looked frantically around and inside it. No Titus. Anywhere. My next thought was that we needed to call 911. It had been 20 minutes and there was no trace of him. I closed my eyes and prayed, "Jesus, you know where he is, please show us." As I opened my eyes, I looked up to see a few lights on in the two story church building. Then I saw movement in the lit stairwell. There he was, sitting in the stairwell. I ran to the double doors in front of me and got through to the foyer. I took a turn towards the stairwell, ran down the long hall to a doorway at the end labeled STAIRS. I pulled open the heavy door and ran up the first flight.

There he was, sitting on the landing above me: "Hi Mama."

"Hi Titus. I have been looking for you. I am so glad I found you." I sat down beside him and gave him a big hug as Aaron appeared on the stairs below.

We took his little hands in ours, catching our breath.

"We found him, he's here! He's here! We found him!" we announced as we walked back to the gym with Titus, alerting everyone who had been frantically searching.

As we got back to the gym, Aaron gathered Titus into his arms and gave him the biggest hug. I wrapped my arms around the two of them, letting tears flow in relief. Just then young Rachael came into the gym, and seeing us with Titus, she started crying as well. It was an unforgettable moment of terror and joy for all of us. She apologized profusely but we told her over and over that it wasn't her fault. We had a very smart child who had waited and watched for his opportunity.

Aaron: What I remember clearly about this night was that we started out with a typical response. We panicked like every other parents would do. I ran into the parking lot and was looking in the shadows for the first few minutes. Then a moment of clarity came. "This kid doesn't hide or go into dark unknown places. What does this kid do? Buttons, he likes buttons, buttons that open doors, buttons that open elevators, buttons that..." It was then that I followed the well lit path around the church to the doors that we always came in on, the doors with the handicapped button for automatically opening the doors. And just inside? A button for calling the elevator. All of the other doors for getting up the stairs to the upper level were locked, but the elevator button worked. So I rode the elevator up to the next level. The elevator opened up into a long hallway, where at the end was another button, one to open the doors to the stairwell. I found the two of them just moments after Karen had found him, sitting on the stairs in a hug.

Rachael: Even to this day, remembering this event makes my heart race and feelings of guilt come rushing back. As a parent now myself I have a whole new perspective on the panic, terror and forgiveness that Aaron and Karen had that night:

The gym was a picture of organized chaos as over a dozen children played various games with happy shrieks and laughter. I was overseeing the high schoolers that were helping out and it was my job to have activities for the kids, but my main responsibility was Titus. I knew the little guy well, and had built a trusting relationship with him through Sunday school and babysitting him and his siblings at their home. I knew that the little man was not to be underestimated and needed constant supervision as he was always on the move with curiosity. I saw him go over to the drinking fountain (a fascinating contraption for his active mind with fun buttons to push that produced water!), then looked away to survey the group of kids playing. When I looked back to the water fountain, Titus was no where to be seen! My heart sank to the pit of my stomach and I quickly scanned the open gym for my little friend. It took only a moment to realize he was no longer in the room. I immediately sent someone to notify Karen and Aaron and our search began. Tearfully I explained to them what had happened. The closest door to the water fountain lead right outside, so we headed outdoors to begin our search in earnest. I somehow had a flashlight and remember splitting up as some people searched the parking lot and church grounds while myself and a few others combed the nearby neighborhood streets. "Titus! Titus where are you?" I shouted, trying to keep the panic out of my voice as to not scare him. I have no idea how long we walked up and down those dark streets as time felt like it was at a stand-still. I kept asking myself how I would ever look the Haslems in the eye again after this. I had failed them after they had entrusted their most precious son into my care. I prayed as hard as I knew how that God would keep that little boy safe and lead us right to him. Soon the word spread that he had been found by his parents in a stairwell! He had found the elevator and taken a little joy ride. Of course! Buttons! His favorite thing! Relief rushed over me but did not wash away my feelings of guilt. I didn't know what to say to Aaron and Karen except to apologize profusely. They were more gracious than I felt I deserved and showered me with compassion and forgiveness. While it took me a while to forgive myself, Titus had been found safe and sound and that was all that mattered.

In May of the end of his second year of preschool, we prepared to attend Kindergarten Round-Up at the school Titus was to attend in the fall. Titus always had a sweet smile and that was all he needed to make a great first impression that afternoon. Titus and I walked into the lobby of the tiny school a few minutes early to allow him extra time to get used to the surroundings before the chaos of the meeting. As we were waiting, a woman walked down the hall toward us.

"Well, hi there! This must be one of my new kindergarten guys!" she said brightly as she bent down to meet Titus. "And what is your name?" Titus looked at his shoes and started jumping up and down.

"This is Titus. He is so happy to be here," I answered cheerfully.

At my answer, her whole countenance changed. She stood straight up and took a step back. "Oh... so *this* is my special needs one."

Another family arrived at that moment and she greeted them warmly and escorted them down the hall towards the classroom. I took Titus by the hand and followed, trying to look past my unflattering first impression of the teacher. We arrived in the bright little kindergarten room and took a few minutes to look it over before more families arrived. There were lots of wonderful things to look at and explore in the room: colorful books, lots of bright signs and decorations on the walls, a fish tank, a cage with a bunny, and even some chinchillas. The time came for the parents to go to our welcome meeting with the principle in a room down the hall. All the new kindergarteners got to stay behind and have a nice get-to-know-you time in the classroom. I thought to myself, this should be interesting. I don't really remember what was said in the parent meeting that afternoon. My thoughts were in the other room with my son, hoping he was doing well in the new environment. It was much different than his preschool and I wondered how it would turn out. After the meeting I hurried out the door and headed to the kindergarten room once again.

"So, how did he do?" I asked.

"Umm... well, not so great. He just wouldn't sit still for anything. He wouldn't leave my computer alone and kept turning it on and off."

"Ah, yes, he does love computers," I said, smiling down at my brilliant son.

"Oh, well, I am going to have to get rid of my computer then," she said with a sigh. "He likes the fuzzy little animals too. Gosh, I'm thinking I'll have to get rid of those too."

I left that meeting and went home and shared with Aaron what had happened. His response was, "Did you tell her that he likes kids too? She might have to get rid of them."

The last thing we wanted was for our son to be a burden to his kindergarten teacher. He deserved better than that. That weekend we started looking for homes in an area closer to the city of Portland. We found just the right one in the beautiful picturesque town of Forest Grove.

CHAPTER 4

Grandma and the Train Tracks

Forest Grove is a beautiful little Oregon town located about an hour from downtown Portland and an hour from the Pacific Coast. We moved into our new 4-bedroom house in early July. The new house seemed so big at the time, I suppose because the kids were so little in it. The three of them loved to play hide and seek and we made a fort in the closet under the stairs, complete with a tent and a lamp. Titus adjusted to the new surroundings quite well. Soon after we moved in, we decided to make his new room as calming as possible and chose to paint the room sky blue with white clouds. As Aaron and I finished up with the blue paint, we decided to take a break and have lunch. As we were eating we suddenly realized it was a bit too quiet. We looked at each other and quietly headed up the stairs, knowing Titus was in his new room. We peeked in to find him with paintbrush in hand, working diligently on a BIG white cloud.

"Titus, are you painting?"

A huge smile covered his face, as did spots of white paint that trailed all the way down to his shoes.

"You are such a big boy and a great helper."

We joined in on the painting of the clouds and the three of us made a very fun memory that afternoon. Years later, I shed a tear or two as we painted over those clouds in preparing to sell the house.

We set up a meeting with his new kindergarten teacher the week before school started. Mrs. Hudock was such a warm person and had years of experience as a kindergarten teacher. As we met her that morning, she bent down and greeted Titus with a gentle smile and a handshake. She allowed him to explore his new classroom and did not tell him "no" about anything. There were no furry animals in the room that day, just a group of colorful fish who got fed by a delighted little boy. There were bright picture books, little tables and chairs, and a reading area complete with a rocking chair and a cozy rug. We showed him where he would be hanging up his backpack and other belongings. He toured the bathrooms and slid down the big blue slide on the playground. As we were leaving Mrs. Hudock said, "Good-bye Titus. We're going to have so much fun this year." My heart smiled knowing my little man was going to be well cared for.

When the little yellow bus showed up at the house on the first day of school, he was ready to go and could now visualize the surroundings that awaited him. The district wisely decided that it would be best for Titus to have a 1:1 aide to help him stay focused in the classroom. He was mainstreamed into the regular classroom setting that year, to be pulled out only for speech therapy and occupational therapy. Titus also got to swim once a week at the local pool. The kids in the class seemed to adjust to his presence just fine, though at times in trying to initiate play, Titus would engage in head-butting, or throwing chalk dust at unsuspecting little girls. Despite his inappropriate attempts to connect with the other kids, they seemed to like him and those same little girls would follow him around in packs and take turns pushing Titus on the swings at recess.

One of the most significant things that happened in first grade was that Titus developed a couple of real friendships. Bodey and Abigail were both in Titus' kindergarten class that year. Abigail was a shy little red-headed girl who loved Titus and followed him wherever he went. Neither one of them spoke very much so they got along quite well. Bodey was a blonde-headed guy who for some reason was drawn to Titus. His mom told us that Bodey, the son of a soldier serving in Iraq, was a different kid when he was around Titus, a sensitive side of him had blossomed. The three of them spent quite of bit of time together in Kindergarten activities and for the first time Titus was invited to a birthday party. The mother of the birthday girl even called me and asked what kind of games Titus might enjoy playing, and what treats he could and couldn't eat. What are his favorite ones? It means so much to us as parents of special needs children when other families go out of their way to make our children feel included and accepted. Of course in these situations a disability doesn't disappear, but it gives the child exposure to "normal" situations. Just as importantly, it gives other children and families opportunities to see what disability is like. The point here is not to tolerate a disability but to embrace it. In our culture, tolerance is a much talked about issue. But in our family we choose to embrace, not just tolerate it. Embrace someone the way they are, don't just tolerate them. Simple things like birthday parties bring a sense of normality to families, even if it's just for a brief moment in time.

Titus was in one of the best school districts in our area for special needs kids, and there were many services available for him. But many school districts struggle financially and cannot provide even the basic services for the children in their district. Many parents have had to fight for these basic services for their child, some even having gone to court over these rights for their children, only to have the case go on and on while the parents and the child struggle. We feel so fortunate that a 1:1 aide for Titus started during Kindergarten and has been part of his education all the way through junior high school. Many wonderfully talented and caring people have made such a difference in his life in their role as an aide for him. They dealt with Titus on his greatest days and his very bad days. Titus has a built in sixth sense for being able to read people really well. There have only been a couple of individuals that didn't work out. One gal was frightened of Titus and he could sense it. Pushing her buttons became a game for him and she was emotionally and physically exhausted by him. One particular personality clash happened in junior high. He told one aide after two weeks of frustration, "I'm gonna bring a lion to class and he's going to EAT YOU!" For the most part, aides along the way happened to fall in love with our son; he is a bright light to those around him, in the midst of his challenges. Titus has always had so many people in his corner, encouraging him and pulling for him to become the best he can be. Comments we've received over the years from these people have made such an impact on me. They helped me realize that my son was making a positive impact on the world around him. The fact that the words come from those who see him at his worst makes them even more meaningful. Here are some of my favorites:

"I've learned so much having Titus in my room this year. I hope it's been a productive year for him - I look forward to watching him progress next year!"

"I have truly enjoyed working with Titus. He is a GREAT kid. See you next year!"

"What can I say.. I will truly miss Titus. He has grown up so much this year. I will have to admit that he is one of my favorites… you have a wonderful son !!"

"I've enjoyed the time I've spent with Titus. He brings joy to me every day. You have a wonderful son with a very tender heart. I wish Titus the best in his new school."

"I am so proud of Titus, he made great progress this year. We really enjoy working with him."

"I had a great year with Titus. Thank you for sharing him with us."

We owe each of them such a debt of gratitude. I have tried to bless them at least once a year with notes of our thanks along with some homemade goodies; Chocolate goes a long way when gifts of encouragement are in order. During one particularly difficult season for Titus, even chocolate was not enough and we treated a few individuals with a bottle of wine. Real friendships have developed along the way between myself and some of those aides. When you communicate with someone on almost a daily basis about a child whom everyone loves, bonds form. I hope to send each of them a graduation announcement when the time comes.

One interesting visit that fall was from a representative of the county Department of Developmental Disabilities. Referred to us by the school district, she came and met Titus and observed our life in action. We had a brief interview about how things were functioning in our world. During our conversation she made an eye-opening statement:

"Your life is normal to you because you live with autism everyday. You do *a lot* of work to try to keep your family as normal as possible. You put in so much effort and time and dedication; it's a heavy load to bear. It's normal to you because you've been functioning like this for so long. But I have to tell you that normal families don't have to pay this much attention to their kids in order to keep their family functioning. My job is to relieve some of the pressure that is put upon you and help you in any way I can."

By listening to us, she was one of the first people to realize how much effort and dedication it takes to run our life. She was there to help and it was a real blessing. At the time, we were really unaware of services that were available to Titus. As it turned out, we were able to get a year's supply of pull-ups for him, an alarm system for our front door (since Titus still liked to try to escape) and even a specialized bike for him just in time for Christmas. They also provided some much needed respite care, and Aaron and I took a weekend away at the beach. We decided at that point that "normal" was really overrated and we chose not to pursue it.

During the last week of school, Titus decided to find out what happens if you pull the fire alarm. All year long, people had been telling him not to touch it. We've learned over the years that telling Titus not to do something usually means he will find a way to do it. So this day he decided to pull the alarm and see what happens. Extreme noise is what he discovered first. Then a bit of chaos, followed by the gathering of all the kids outside on the playground. Then the big red fire trucks and a police car showed up. The excitement ended with the Fire Chief coming to have a talk with Titus, a very stern talk which ended with Titus in tears. We were happy about the Fire Chief coming down hard: we knew Titus would never pull the fire alarm again. He still remembers the event today.

When a family enters the world of autism, there is an onslaught of information. Information on the specific diagnosis, treatment, and a barrage of therapy choices: play therapy, speech therapy, occupational therapy, chelation therapy, animal therapy, diet changes, ABA therapy, LOVAAS therapy, removal of heavy metals and toxins, the list goes on and on. For many families none of these are realistic options outside of the local school district. Therapy can be very expensive, and at that time very few insurance companies would cover such therapy. When Titus was just diagnosed we did look into intensive ABA therapy. It would have taken over our life: hiring, training, and scheduling therapists, dealing with the cost of supplies and the disruption of our everyday life. The cost would have been over $40,000. We would have been in debt to this day, and not a dime of it would've been covered by insurance. A couple of years later, we looked into ABA therapy again in Oregon. We went to meet a therapist in her very impressive office. Again, the therapy was not covered by insurance, and there was no guarantee that Titus would improve.

Early on, Aaron and I had decided that we wouldn't let the diagnosis of autism rule our lives and the lives of our other children. We didn't think it wise or beneficial for our family to bounce from therapy to therapy, or the myriad of treatments that may or may not work. We didn't want to sacrifice our young family to the pursuit of "curing" one child. We love Titus just the way he is. We didn't want to "fix" our son to the point that he would lose his amazing personality. God chose to give Titus to us the way he is. We'd rather have Titus the way he is, with autism, than to have him without his character. We had to come to the point that having Titus, just the way he was, was okay, including his autism and all that comes with it. Before starting any therapy we had to come to grips with this: if therapy didn't change him, we'd be okay with that. If therapy improves his life and helps him function better, great. Our main focus has been to help him learn to function in the world. One promising therapy that we did feel was worth our investment was Relationship Development Intervention or RDI.

We first found out about RDI at an autism fair at a local health food store. I decided to attend a weekend seminar in Seattle to find out more about the program. It was a very informative session and it was there that I met a woman who was in training to become a certified therapist. She had her own son with autism and we connected immediately. Soon after, we invested in therapy for our son. RDI is a family-based therapy so it took place in our house, led by us, supervised by our therapist who would review taped sessions of our interactions on a bi-weekly basis. We learned how to engage Titus in games and interactions that helped him connect in more meaningful ways. In the 6 months that we engaged in the therapy, Titus made great strides. He began making eye contact and we all learned how to use declarative language and fewer words in our communication. We tried to incorporate the therapy into everyday life. It was therapy without looking like therapy. RDI therapy is not a therapy where the goal is to cure autism, but to help the child adapt to the world.

We tried as best we could to incorporate RDI into the school setting. We sent loads of information about this new therapy and even sat down during an IEP and presented it. Our efforts were generally blocked with comments like "that's not a proven therapy" and "that will never happen here." The one person who really took an interest in RDI was Titus's aide that year. Unfortunately, we as parents apparently crossed an unspoken line when we invited her over for dinner to discuss how she could communicate better with our son. Consequently, she didn't return to the school district the following year. It was a hard lesson for us to learn. In the 6 months that we used RDI with Titus we saw great improvement, but we had to end it for two reasons: our therapist was discontinuing her practice, and early that summer, we found out that we were expecting our fourth miracle baby.

In August of that summer, I decided to take the kids on a road trip to Western Montana to visit my family. I was feeling good in the second trimester of my pregnancy and knew that it would be a long while before I would have the chance to visit again. Aaron was busy at work with a pressing project and couldn't come along. This trip provided one of my most unforgettable experiences with Titus.

Titus in Grandma's back yard in Western Montana.

We had been staying with my mom and stepfather in their cozy little home in the Mission Valley where I grew up. My mother was not used to having her grandchildren there, of course, but treasured every moment with them. Around lunchtime of our second day, my mom decided she needed to get something from the car.

"Titus, come with Grandma. You can help me get something from the car," she said excitedly.

Titus eagerly put his shoes on and took his Grandma's hand.

"We'll be right back, Mommy," she said.

"Titus, you hold Grandma's hand, okay?" I called, figuring they might take a little walk to the mailbox that was just at the end of the dirt driveway. They couldn't go too far, since my mom was wearing her fluffy pink slippers

"Oh, don't worry Mommy, Titus will listen to Grandma so good, won't he?"

I continued to prepare lunch for Noah and Ciciley as I chatted with Papa Roy. I helped the kids pick up their toys so they could take a quick nap after lunch. It had been about 5 minutes since Grandma and Titus had left and my radar system went off.

"I'm going to go check on Grandma and Titus. You guys sit here and eat your lunch."

I stepped outside expecting to find them admiring a colorful geranium or an intriguing statue in Grandma's garden. I didn't see them right away so I walked around to the other side of the house. They were nowhere to be seen.

"Titus, where are you?" I called with a giggle. I thought maybe they were playing hide and seek with me, knowing I would be looking.

"Titus, come out now. It's lunch time!" I called again. I walked all around the house, my eyes quickly scanning the one-acre property. There was no sign of Titus, and no sign of my mom.

Panic hit me and I quickly ran into the house. "Roy, can you stay here with the little ones? I'm going to go look." Roy was a big gentle bear of a man who was a WWII vet. Those day his knees weren't up to chasing after a 6 year old. I didn't want to alarm Noah and Ciciley and knew they'd be happy to stay with Papa Roy. I grabbed my car keys, ran outside and jumped into the car. As I went to turn the key I stopped and prayed, "Jesus, you know where my son is. Please, please keep him safe."

My mom and Roy lived about two miles from town in a rural area. Dusty dirt roads lined the landscape amid the horse and cattle farms in the area. I pulled out of the driveway and onto the road. Calling out his name from the opened windows every few feet, I drove slowly, crossing railroad tracks and venturing about a mile down the dusty road. Houses and yards and open fields went by. I even stopped by one house that was closer to the road. I ran to the front door and knocked. The gentleman inside must have thought I was crazy when I asked him if he'd seen a little boy and a Grandma type walk by. He shook his head kindly and closed the door. I got in the car again and drove back towards the house, my heart racing.

Picking up my cell phone, I called my brother who happened to work just 5 minutes away. "I can't find Titus or Mom. I need help. Can you come?" my voice trembling.

I drove slowly past the house again, searching for them. I drove up the road the other direction towards the main highway that led into town, focusing on the big ditch that ran along the outside of the property. I turned around again and retraced the road that I had been searching along, this time going a bit further. Going another mile past where I'd gone before, tears rolling down my cheeks, I continued to pray. At that point, it must have been about an hour since they had both disappeared. I needed to call 911. Just at that moment I spotted 3 figures in the distance. As I drove closer I saw that it was my brother with Titus in his arms and my exhausted mother following behind. As I got out of the car and started toward them relief hit me in a wave. Sobbing, I doubled over in pain as my lungs tightened and my growing tummy tightened up in a contraction. Knowing I needed to calm myself before I talked to Titus, I took a few deep breaths. Titus happily ran towards me and gave me a big hug. As I hugged him I couldn't hold back the sobs. Looking up I saw my mother crying as well, as my brother held her hand.

"Hi Mama. Grandma chased me." he said happily as he looked at my tear-stained face.

"Hi Titus. I am SO GLAD to see you. Are you okay?" I attempted a happy face and a clear voice.

"I just let go of his hand for a second. He just took off." My mom spoke through her tears as she hugged me.

"I know Mom, it's not your fault. He thought it was a game," I said, trying to reassure her.

"We were walking by the car and I let go of his hand so I could open the door. The minute I let go he was off toward the mailbox. I called to him to come back but he wouldn't listen. He wouldn't come back so I just decided I should follow him and he'd stop at the mailbox.

But he just kept running! I thought I should at least see where he was running to."

I looked down at her slippers, no longer pink but dusty brown and tattered.

"Why didn't you just come and get me?" I voiced my wonder.

"All I could think was that I needed to keep him safe." It was then that I remembered that my mother is a mother too.

Titus had indeed run past the mailbox and down the road that I had driven on. When he got to the railroad tracks he hopped on them and managed to run another mile down the track, my poor mother in her pink slippers trying desperately to keep up. He ran and ran until he came to a bridge high above a ravine below. He stopped and sat down on the edge and as my mom approached him he was throwing rocks into the water below.

"You caught me!" he said innocently as his grandma approached him, out of breath. Just as she reached him my brother, Fred, ran up behind them. My brother told me later, "you don't want to know where I found him." To this day I've never gone to that spot.

"Hi Titus, we need to go find your Mom," he said as he gathered Titus into his arms.

Fred: I remember being at Dad's house about 10 minutes away when Karen called, frantic and almost crying. She was at Mom's house with her kids, and somehow Mom and Titus had disappeared suddenly. She asked me to please come over to Mom's right away. I think she had her two younger kids with her also and really could not go too far to look for Mom and Titus. I think I had one of my boys with me, we raced over on the back roads, and ran into the house to see if any progress had been made. Karen was frantic. I think I remember praying with Karen very quickly then jumping back in the car to go look. It was a very hot and sunny day. I took off in the truck and headed west really not knowing how to even begin searching. I drove maybe a hundred yards west down the road past the railroad tracks, and beyond the tracks maybe another 50 yards... the tracks! Titus would love the straight lines of the railroad tracks! I backed up to be right on top of the tracks and looked south straight down the RR tracks. Way, way down the tracks, at least 3/4 of a mile, I could see movement on the tracks... two people, one large, one small... it had to be them I took off on a dead run down the tracks toward the figures. The closer I got I could tell for sure it was mom and Titus. She was holding his hand tight, and he was trying to get away from her grip. She was covered in sweat and out of breath, with a very scared and frustrated look on her face. The look on Titus' face was a smile. To him it was a fun game with Grandma. As soon as I got to them, I grabbed Titus and held him. He was laughing and squirming in my arms. Mom sat down on the ground, very tired but very relieved. I let her sit for a few minutes as she told me what had happened. Titus had headed out the door, and Mom, knowing his love of escaping, went after him. To him it was a game, and Grandma was playing. She came very near to catching him several times, but finally got to him what turned out to be about a mile and a half away. What a day.

The whole incident left me shaken for hours and I wasn't able to call Aaron for awhile.

"Guess what *your* son did today?"

I described the event of the day, still shaken up a bit. After my call I decided to wait an extra day to make the six hour drive to Billings to see Aaron's parents. I was glad I did as I woke up the next day exhausted and very sore all over. Ever since then, when I go through a difficult time with Titus emotionally, my body reacts in a physical way. For this reason, Aaron is usually the one who handles a stressful issue at home.

CHAPTER 5

Change Is Good

That summer we celebrated Titus's birthday at a party with his two best friends, special helium balloons and a jungle animal theme. A few days later, after much warning about the consequences, Titus let his balloons go outside. Crying immediately at the sight of his balloons going far, far away he came to me wanting me to "fix it." The Super Mom that he envisioned me to be could not leap tall buildings to fetch them.

"Oh Titus, I told you that the balloons would go high up in the sky if you let them go. Mom can't get them back."

He continued to be more and more upset, not understanding why I, the all powerful mother, could not fix his dilemma. After an hour or so of listening to his crying I came up with a solution.

"Hey Titus, you know what I just thought of? The astronauts way up in the sky will be so happy to see your birthday balloons." A big smile came across his face, the crying stopped and contentment appeared.

Later that summer, we attempted once again to teach Titus how to ride a bike. He just didn't have the hand-eye coordination and the gross motor skills needed. We had tried big wheels, tricycles, training wheels: he just never seemed to figure out how to get the vehicle to move. Then we had an eye-opening experience. The Lance Armstrong Livestrong Ride was meandering through and around our little town that particular weekend. We went out that Sunday morning to cheer the riders on. The kids lined the road holding US Flags shouting, "Good job, way to go!" to each rider that went by. A little while later a father-son combination went riding by on what we found out was a trail-along bike. Watching this father-son combination made us wonder about the possibility. Titus could pedal, shift gears, and everything else while watching a model demonstration right in front of him. Plus, Mom or Dad riding in front made the bike balance so he could focus on the pedaling. Later that afternoon we went to a local bike shop and queried the shop owner about such a bike. Expensive was the price at $150 and so my thrift-seeking husband prayed and then headed to his favorite hang out: the local Goodwill store.

Aaron: The next weekend we casually went to the local Goodwill. Honestly, I didn't expect to find such a cool treasure, we were just out to scan the aisles. But there it was, practically brand new, no scratches, good grips, good seat, chain was still oily. The only thing missing was the collar for attaching it to the lead bike. God's price tag, $30. The local bike tinkerer had the collar, he never puts price tags on anything so he asked if $12 would do. Ti and I mounted up when we got home, we took a short ride up and down the street while mom and the kids cheered Titus on for his first bike ride. When we pulled up to the curb Ti sweetly proclaimed, "Ok Mommy's turn." From his perspective he had been giving me a ride up and down the street. Now that's a way to build confidence.

Late in the summer, Titus began a normal ritual for every child: losing his baby teeth. Most children love this aspect of childhood and can understand the reason for it and the literal pay off under their pillow. Titus did not react so well. He would ask for a glue stick wanting to fix the loose tooth. We decided to pull his first tooth out because it had become a real distraction for him, so much so that he was not wanting to eat.

We pulled it out as it was hanging on by the last root.

"Oh boy Titus, look at that! You lost your first tooth!" Dad said as he held up the bloody tooth for Titus to see.

"PUT IT BACK! PUT IT BACK!" he screamed, tears squeezing out of his eyes. "It's okay buddy, another big tooth will grow in soon!" we tried to reassure him.

He looked in the bathroom mirror, still crying, took one look at the hole the missing tooth had left and started screaming all over again. This wasn't a normal "I'm sad" kind of cry. This became unconsollable sobbing until he wore himself out two hours later and fell asleep. The pile of quarters awaiting him the next morning seemed to ease his sheer misery as we visited the local grocery store and he got a handful of his favorite colorful gum balls.

We had similar experiences with hair cuts. When he was just a toddler I had taken him to a cute little children's hair salon for a haircut. He got to sit in a cool airplane chair that went up and down. It had endless buttons and gadgets that delighted the little man as he barely noticed his hair was being cut. I had cut his hair a few times when he was a baby with no problems, just handfuls of fish crackers and a video to appease him. Little snips here and there as I could while he sat still. But by the time he was five, having his hair cut became a bigger issue. He couldn't stand to have the little snips of hair on him and the sound of the clippers unnerved him. The session would take a long time and he would cry the whole time saying, "Be done, BE DONE." As he's matured over the years he's learned how to deal with a haircut from Mom, but he *really* loves going to the salon to get the full treatment. The trick is finding a stylist who is patient enough to answer all his questions and embrace his quirkiness. Being that he's a young man now, I really think he loves the attention he gets from those pretty girls.

At the beginning of his first grade year, Titus did pretty well adjusting to the newness of everything; new classroom, new teacher, new aide, new kids to get to know. Many times over the years I have called my sister, Cindy, to share experiences, the good and not so good.

Cindy: When Karen called me I wasn't sure if she was laughing or crying; happy or sad. Her voice was happy, but it had a kind of trembling, too. She called to tell me the latest about Titus, something she often called me about. We would talk and laugh, and sometimes get real serious. Titus was in the first grade, and had just gotten on the bus to go to school. She explained how he always got on and sat down, looking straight ahead as the bus began to move. But today was different. Her voice broke as she told me that he turned around and waved goodbye! It was a first, a milestone. A glimmer of love. He had not connected emotionally since he was diagnosed. I imagined the scene, what he was wearing, his bright little face, a red shirt, looking back at my precious sister as she smiled back and waved. I still see the imagined scene as clear as the day it happened. It was a very happy day.

His reading skills were more developed at this point as well. He had learned how to read by sight after a trial and error period by the staff. They tried to teach him phonetically along with the rest of the class but then discovered his amazing visual learning style. After a few weeks of pulling him out with a gifted one on one reading aide who taught him sight words, he was caught up to the rest of his classmates. He could read words and was speaking more and more, but those who didn't know him well had a difficult time understanding him. His speech therapy continued with a more intense focus on pronunciation of sounds. His classroom teacher was ever so accepting of Titus. He told us one day that Titus had climbed under his chair during class while all the other kids were on the floor. "He looked up at me… I just let him stay there. I figured he was quiet and it was less of a disruption than trying to get him to sit with the others. He's mostly a quirky kid, but I *like* Titus." This particular 1st grade teacher had found that it was easier to have him quirky than force him to sit still. Acceptance.

Early in the year, Titus would have problems coping in certain situations. He started day two by checking out the drinking fountain and then proceeded to spit the water all over the floor. He also started head-butting and being aggressive on the playground. We never saw these behaviors at home, so we knew the environment at school was especially challenging for him; he was trying to gain some control in any way he could. These sorts of behaviors continued on a daily basis and the staff was at a loss. We decided to give them a little lesson on how to communicate with Titus. One aspect of dealing with Titus is the need to be firm. He was such a cute little guy that most people, upon meeting him, wouldn't want to speak a harsh word to him. But Titus reads <u>all</u> the communication signs: body language first, then tone of voice, then the words you say. So if you want him to follow a direction or take correction you must *not* smile sweetly and use a sweet voice. Firm is best with very few words. We gave the staff a visual demonstration on how to correct him: use a mean face and your "Mom" voice. On the flip side, when he does something great, get really excited and happy. Over exaggerate your response with high fives and great big smiles! As a family we had learned this type of communication and our other three children are professionals.

The gym was certainly not Titus's favorite place: the echoing sounds really bothered him and the staff saw escalations in behavior as he attempted to function in this overwhelming environment. One of his coping mechanisms was to run. Titus has always been a gifted runner, but it's not the greatest gift for a 6 year old who's trying to escape or the person who's trying to keep up with him. We started to get alarming notes in the communication manual:

"Titus ran away from staff today, but it's okay, the other students caught him."

"Titus ran out of the classroom today for no reason."

"Titus ran out of PE again today."

"He wanders off to other places in the building if we don't watch him carefully."

These kind of messages would send fear through me, just imagining what might happen to him at school if no one did catch him. I sent him off to school each day on the bus, whispering a prayer that God would keep him safe from harm. Up to this point, no harm has ever come to him, but we always had to warn new staff: get your running shoes ready.

As Titus was getting his running done at school, I was running around at home preparing for our new baby to arrive that January. Noah and Ciciley were at home and kept me busy with their daily needs as well. Baby number four had been a complete surprise as we had finally been using birth control, which thankfully didn't work. We had even gotten rid of all of our baby items the year before, as well as all my maternity clothes. Titus seemed especially interested in the baby and my growing tummy. He'd been around for my previous two pregnancies but at 7 years old he was more curious than ever before. When we had an ultrasound done he took the little picture to school for sharing time. He didn't "share" much about it except to say "baby" with a big smile. At the beginning of the year standing up in front of the class was not something he did well. He wouldn't say a word and wouldn't make much eye contact. But the more he shared about *his* new baby, the more he started to enjoy the experience and the attention from his classmates. He began to make good eye contact and say a few words. By the end of first grade, he was standing a bit taller and even taking questions from his classmates. His curiosity about the baby peaked at home as my tummy got bigger and bigger. He didn't understand why he couldn't see the baby. Several times he would lift up my shirt and try to look through my belly button so he could "see baby." These episodes were new and unexpected but I was so happy that he was already making a connection with his new brother or sister.

We had some fun adventures as a family during this time. In November we decided to attempt taking the whole family to see *The Lion King* on Broadway when it came to downtown Portland. We decided to bring along Miss Rachael from church for reinforcement with our little troop. All three of the kids were enthralled from the moment the curtain opened until the music stopped at the end. After the show we purchased a CD of music from the show and for weeks afterward, Noah and Ciciley would reenact it all with their little animals.

That Christmas we welcomed Aaron's father, his brother and his wife, and their young daughters. The house was a bustle of activity and fun until all of us got a flu bug. It was 48 hours of potty trips and cleaning of sheets. I watched everyone else get sick and thought my immune system was ultra powerful in pregnancy. It wasn't to be, of course, and dehydration from the bug sent me into contractions and a trip to the hospital thinking I was in labor. Our little one decided to wait until the very last minute to arrive: on my due date when I had to be induced.

Knowing that I was going to be induced, we were able to let the kids know that the new baby would be arriving the next day. We left the house early in the morning as a close friend of ours came to stay with the younger two. Titus had been anxious all week but on that day in school he was overly agitated and not able to focus. He constantly mentioned "Mommy and baby" throughout the day. It was truly heartwarming to know that he was so concerned about me. It wasn't just me that felt the bond, he obviously felt it too. Titus never said "I love you," so his reaction to me being in the hospital was very reassuring. Our third son, Lucas, arrived that evening, a healthy 9 pound 3 ounce baby. He has truly been a delight from the moment we saw him. Titus went to school the next day and excitedly shared the news that *his* new baby brother had arrived. After school that day, Daddy gathered him off the bus and the four of them headed to the hospital. Titus was more excited than anyone as he got to hold his new little brother and look into his eyes. He was in awe. It was amazing to see him react this way, it felt a little bit like normal. He certainly loved his new brother but had a hard time at school during the transition. For about two weeks afterward he had potty accidents, possibly because he couldn't really understand his feelings about all the changes at home.

Titus looking so proud, holding his new baby brother Lucas.

One of the really amazing aspects of that year was the Zoo Walk for Autism at the Portland Zoo. We told the kids that we all got to go to the zoo because Titus was so cool and we were getting in for free because of him! We made up matching green T-shirts with Titus' photo on the front and headed off for a day at the zoo, not knowing what God had in store for us. From the moment we arrived in the busy parking lot we saw that there were loads of families just like ours. We saw other parents with advanced radar systems helping their kids across the busy parking lots. Gluten free snacks were everywhere as well. The crowds that day were rather large but the most impressive part was that all of us understood each other. Titus and every other kid with autism in attendance that day could be themselves and no one would be staring. There would be no strangers wondering about the freakish kid. There would be no pointing fingers from innocent little ones asking questions. Early on in the day we were walking along with the crowd through a tunnel when we heard a frantic mom, "Stop him, Stop him!" Seconds later a fast little boy was stopped by a man ahead of us. In that moment we knew that we were in a crowd that we fit in.

We decided to take a ride on the zoo train that meanders slowly around the zoo and the adjacent park. It was a beautiful ride visually but even more so, I felt it was a little gift from God. I sat next to another mom with whom Ciciley struck up a conversation by asking "Is that your son? Does he have autism too?" The woman and I immediately struck up a conversation about our boys. Being that we were on the same journey, there was already understanding and the superficial aspect of meeting someone new was not present. We both drank deep in the frank conversation about the issues we faced as mothers of boys with autism. We chatted about special diets, potty training, inappropriate behaviors at school, the non-dating aspect of marriage, and how siblings are handling life. We were in agreement about how our other children were becoming amazing people because of their sibling who had autism. It was only a 15 minute conversation, but so valuable because for the first time I realized that someone else knew exactly what my life was like on a daily basis. We never connected again, but I won't soon forget the impact it had. There *were* other moms out there who had the same kind of days that I had. *I was not alone.*

I remember too that day seeing a couple standing in line for tickets. With them was a tall, slender teen-ager who must have been about 17. Looking back, I wish I would have approached them and asked a few questions. Their son was obviously on the spectrum but functioning on a very high level. He spoke well and communicated his needs appropriately as he purchased the tickets. At that moment I wondered how we would ever get to that place with Titus. What would our little boy look like at 17? How would he function? Where would he be academically? Would he have friends? What would his life be like at 17? So many questions and no answers. But looking at this couple who were further down the path than we provided some hope as well as the thought provoking questions. Having a child with autism is full of unknowns. For us, the only thing we could do was give it all to Jesus. It sounds cliche' but that is what we have had to do to get through. I don't know the future of my son, but I know who holds his future. God holds his future and I get to trust that it's good. We had some good friends ask us around this time what our plan was when Titus became an adult. That question has the potential to be quite overwhelming. If we didn't have the solid assurance that God holds the plans, I'm not sure how we'd get through our journey. Ever since I saw that couple in the zoo that day, I always encourage people to ASK QUESTIONS. Never hesitate to ask us anything. We want to encourage other families on this road.

Having a child with special needs can put strain on a marriage. As for our relationship, I can honestly say we've grown stronger individually and closer as a couple. A huge part of that is a sense of humor. Some days, the only thing we can do is shake our heads and laugh. It's not helpful to stress and worry about something we can't change. We do support each other through the rough patches and thankfully it's been balanced out; most of the time we don't both have a rough day on the same day. Unfortunately, dating is not something we are able to do often. We have tried over the years to plan for big events such as anniversaries. But family is far away and not able to commit, and we'd like to keep our friends and not take advantage of them. We have had a handful of dates over the years, but Titus has given the babysitters challenges. Like most kids, he tries to get away with things with a sitter around. Once when a young man from across the street was watching the kids, Titus decided to throw his vitamins all over the floor and dump the rest of the bottle out. Another time, after being told it was bedtime, he bolted out the front door in his pajamas and ran down the street giggling. One other evening Titus snuck out of the room during reading time and poured baby powder all over the bathroom floor. As the kids have gotten older, Noah has been able to handle his brother's antics and we do get away for an evening once in awhile. Thankfully, we are able to spend most evenings together and pop in a movie or read. In our relationship a closeness has been achieved that could've only been formed in the fire of what we've been through together.

Aaron and I - Mt. Hood in the background.

In first grade, Titus started having elevated behavior issues in the spring. Since that year, every spring has brought a sort of upheaval in our son's life. It may have to do with knowing that a big change, summer, is coming. First grade in the spring was difficult for Titus. He would get upset and spit on the walls and the floor, a behavior he learned on the bus. He had a meltdown about every other day, featuring new behaviors such as taking his clothes off in class, taking his clothes off in the time out space, and even flushing his feet in the urinal. As the end of the year got closer, his behaviors escalated and he spent most of his time outside of the classroom. Part of the problem may have been that while he was spending time outside the classroom, he was getting pretzels from one of staff who was apparently unaware that Titus was allergic to gluten, even though we had it written on big, bold, red letters on his paperwork and stressed it so often. The staff member's response was "he just had a few." I suppose the lesson was learned that "just a few" was just too many.

Early that summer an article came out in the local paper about an international exchange program for students at the nearby college. Host families were needed. Aaron brought it to me and giggled. I took one look at the headline and said, "That sounds really interesting. We should look into it." His jaw dropped as he looked at me holding our 6 month old baby while wiping the hands of our two year old daughter. Here again, we try very hard not to let autism rule our lives, or the lives of our other 3 children. We could've decided that our life was too busy or too challenging to invest in new experiences. Yet we felt that an opportunity to meet people from another part of the world would be of great benefit to our children. I grew up in a small town in Montana and had few opportunities to experience other cultures. As a family, we didn't have the means to travel to other countries, so the thought of bringing other cultures into our home was very appealing. As a result, that summer we hosted our first student for 6 weeks. He barely spoke English and Noah especially delighted in teaching him the names of all sorts of things around the house. The kids loved having someone new around to play with and the students in turn loved our kids. Over the years we've hosted an array of students. Some stayed for 2 weeks, some stayed for 9 months. We've hosted young men and women from Saudi Arabia, Japan, China, and Korea. Many of them still keep in touch with us today. An interesting aspect of this adventure was explaining autism to our house guests. Most of them understood once they punched the word "autism" into their state of the art hand-held dictionaries. One student from China had a particularly memorable response. I had just explained to her that Titus had autism.

"Do you understand autism?" I asked.

Her English was exceedingly good as she was a graduate student. "Oh yes. I know all about autism. Did you know that the reason he has autism is because you didn't hold him enough when he was a baby?"

I laughed, "Oh, no. It's not. That is such an old idea. Where did you learn that?"

"I learned all about it in secondary school. It's a very good school," she stated matter of factly.

"Well, the information is outdated. Autism has nothing to do with the care of the mother. His brain is different."

I could tell that she didn't believe me and wanted to hold on to her own belief about the issue. Later that week, she tried to tell me how to potty train Lucas. Needless to say, she didn't stay much longer.

Thanksgiving that fall was one of the most memorable we've ever had. Most of the time, our families are not able to be with us on holidays, so we invite as many people as we can who also have no family living close. On this particular holiday we had a houseful of 22 guests, including some of our exchange students and some of their family and friends, as well as some of our closest friends. The lovely people who sat at our table that year represented six different countries: America, Japan, Saudi Arabia, India, Bulgaria, and Korea; as well as four different religions: Christian, Buddhist, Hindu, and Muslim. It was truly a blessed day and an unforgettable experience for our family as well as our guests. What a gift it was to bring the world into our home. In the midst of having these new people in and out of the house, Titus learned critical lessons about changes. He adjusted to them well as long as we supported him with the information beforehand. For Titus, change is never the problem. The problem is unpredictable chaos. Having exchange students rotating in and out of our home became a routine occurrence, and we were able to teach him that change is a *good* thing. When change happened, he was prepared. These critical lessons served him well later on as we made more momentous life changes.

CHAPTER 6

Very Literal

Second grade was a season of difficult days for Titus and everyone around him. As always he was excited to begin school that fall, but within the first week he started having issues. Seemingly little things would set him off: a jigsaw puzzle missing a piece, his zipper getting stuck in his coat, falling down in the mud, and the wind whipping around him on the playground. These occurrences sent him into fits of frustration; it would take him two hours to calm down. We began to see more aggressive behavior as he hit classmates, his speech therapist, and even his best friend for no apparent reason. He also regressed in terms of his toileting habits, having several accidents. The staff at the school was so very patient and they tried everything they could to alleviate his turmoil. The autism specialist in the district suggested some options. Titus started wearing a special sensory vest during the day. A sensory vest is a weighted vest which allowed him to feel like he was getting a comforting hug from the compression of the vest. He was afforded more sensory breaks and given special sensory toys to play with to relieve some of his anxiety and calm him. He was also given deep pressure massage when needed. The staff created a "safe space" outside of the classroom where he could go to calm down. The space was essentially a small, soft, quiet area where he could have a meltdown without hurting himself or someone else. During the day, if his aide felt that he was getting agitated, she would take him for a quick walk around the building to release some of his anxiety.

We knew he was having a hard time at school. Some days after school he would walk in the door, ask for a snack and as I was preparing one, fall asleep at the table. One aspect of his behavior that I have been thankful about over the years is that he has never once been aggressive with Aaron or me or his siblings. Because of this, his behavior was somewhat baffling to the staff. We knew that home for him was a calm and safe place; school for Titus was an onslaught of significant challenges on a daily basis.

Though his year started out with some rough patches, when he was able to function in the classroom Titus did very well on the actual school work. His reading was right at grade level as were most of his language arts skills, and he understood the basic math skills being presented. Titus learned some very positive things. After months of working on it, he finally started to greet people without being prompted. Normally he wouldn't say hello to a teacher or anyone else without being reminded to do so. This is a courtesy that is often taken for granted as neurotypical children learn it easily. He also started saying "please" and "thank you" on his own. Again, these are very important social skills which took loads of work. I still get comments today on how polite my son is. I have all the people who worked so intensively with him in those early years to thank for it.

Another positive aspect added to his education was the use of the computer in class. Since he was such a visual learner, Titus was able to use certain educational games in school as part of his lessons in math and language arts. Additional computer time became a positive reinforcement for good behavior. This reinforcement became more and more important as he got older. From the time he was four years old Titus has loved the computer and been very well versed in how to work it. He would sit on his daddy's lap and just watch and learn. In fact, he was so good at the computer that it took him five minutes unattended at Grandpa Skogen's computer to shut down the internet when he was only 6 years old. $86 and days after we had left, it was fixed. Nowadays, if there is ever an issue with a computer at home, Titus can usually fix it.

The staff at the school also changed the way Titus met his Physical Education requirement. They placed him in an amazing adaptive PE program. Adaptive PE is a special physical education setting where kids with disabilities pick a "buddy" who comes along with them during the class. Buddies are neurotypical kids who understand that they are there to help their friend with a disability to learn a skill. The kids would learn all sorts of games and skills as well as how to interact socially in a different setting than the classroom. The program benefits not only a child with a disability but also the neurotypical kids who get to learn how children with a disability function. This kind of interaction is so beneficial in developing mutual respect as children grow into adults. I wish every school had such a wonderful program. Titus also continued his swimming program each week. Every Friday he looked forward to going to the pool with other special needs kids and the amazing teachers who ran the program. The kids would not only focus on swimming but also other aquatic exercises and social interaction through game time in the pool.

Thanksgiving that year was once again a special adventure for our family. Living so close, the Pacific Ocean was always a draw, but the cost of accommodations for six of us was not usually in the budget. This particular time we decided to rent a cozy house near the beach, a rate that was cheaper than 4 nights in a hotel. We decided to take two of our favorite exchange daughters from Japan, Satomi and Yuki, as well as two of our dearest friends - Wally and Shirley. We met Wally and Shirley at a couple's meeting at our church and became fast friends; even though they are a generation or two ahead of us, we have much in common. With our kids' grandparents not able or not willing to visit our family, God has filled the gap that our kids needed and longed for. So in a real sense we spent that week with our family, and it was an amazing time of relaxation and fun.

Our family at the beach house.

On day three, while we were all playing a game, Titus decided to sneak upstairs and spice things up a bit by making a prank call to 911. He had done it once before at home and he had gotten a consequence for his behavior but it obviously wasn't enough to keep him from doing it again.

It was about this time that Titus developed a love for Pixar movies and digital animation. He would center on what we called a "movie of the week." He'd put in a chosen Pixar movie after school each day and just relax. He would put the same movie in the next day, and the next, all the way through the week. It was and continues to be something that he can control and predict. We believe Titus has a photographic memory. He has a wealth of knowledge about Pixar, both the movies and the company. He can tell you the name of every character of every movie, the year it was made, and who directed it. If asked, he could probably quote scenes word for word.

Titus came to me one day when he was in eighth grade wanting me to give him John Lasseter's address, like I would actually have the address for the CEO of Pixar Animation studios. Of course he was incensed that I didn't have it in my address book. "Why don't you have it, Mom? You know John Lasseter, don't you?" I loved the fact that he thought I knew everything.

"Well, Titus, I know who John Lasseter is, but I don't KNOW him. Why would I have his address?"

"Okay then Mom, it's okay that you don't have his address. We can just look it up on the internet!" he said, jumping up and down with excitement.

"Ummm, it's not that easy Titus, people like John Lasseter don't just post their address on the internet for everyone to see," I said, trying to explain all this so he would somehow understand.

He looked at me with a shocked expression. "What? Why not? Doesn't he know that people want to visit him?"

"Titus, how would you feel if people came over to your house, uninvited, all the time to visit you and ask you questions about your creations?" I said, trying to get him to understand this concept.

"I WOULD LOVE IT, and John Lasseter will too! Can we please get his address?" Of course he would. I had to give up at this point and say, "I'll have to find that address some other time, how about in October of 2015?"

Unfortunately Pixar doesn't give tours of their facility and I've attempted to contact them several times about a special tour to encourage my son, but alas, they are too busy making more great films.

A particularly interesting quality about Titus, and many kids on the spectrum, is that he is very literal. One fall evening as I was prepping dinner Titus came and asked, "Can I go outside?"

"No Titus, it's almost dinnertime and it's getting dark out."

Ignoring that response, Titus started towards the door. "Where are you going, Ti?" Aaron asked.

"I'm going outside." he said matter-of-factly, his hand on the door handle.

"I told you no, Titus." Aaron stood up, hands in his pockets.

"Why?" said Titus.

"Because I said so," replied Aaron in his firm Dad voice.

"SO," Titus replied, and he promptly opened the door and walked outside.

Aaron and I just looked at each other for a moment in surprise. What had just happened? I think we realized once again how smart our young son was and how carefully we had to use language.

Aaron: I was amazed today with a comment a close colleague of mine made on an observation. I was relaying to him the story of a rather heated discussion I had with one of our executives.

Let me put in a side note, I have been feeling a bit of anxiety and contention lately. So much so that this colleague, and others that know me, have begun coming to my desk when they need a good devil's advocate to practice presenting a proposal, or a better understanding of an issue that they are contending... in other words, right now at least, they know I will help them wrestle with their ideas, topic is not an issue.

Needless to say, my story about arguing with one of our executives did not surprise my colleague.

Here's the argument in a nutshell. This executive had asked me how something could be done better, being an engineer, everything can always be done better. But then this executive asked me to figure out how to fix a problem we are having by giving me instructions on a method he wanted me to investigate and figure out how to implement his method to fix the problem. A month later (the request was made during a monthly meeting) I reported that there were fundamental obstacles in the way and I was not finding a way to implement his method. I told him that I did not think implementing his method was possible. His response was that I should return the following month with more action than having "just thought about it." I snapped. I told this executive that his instructions for me were to find a way to implement his method, HOW, not IF it could be implemented. I was making it clear that he had specifically asked for me to find out HOW to implement his method, not IF it could be implemented. I then made it clear that I was still struggling with the IF portion of the problem because I was not finding a clear answer to even IF his method was possible let alone, HOW. Thus my results were incomplete because I was not there to report IF his method could be implemented, I was asked to show HOW his method could be implemented. Since I had not found a clear resolution to IF it was even possible, I had not and was not prepared to answer HOW. (I know this is repetitive, but I wanted it to be very clear that I was dissecting his request.)

As I relayed this story to my colleague he began to smile in amazement. I have told this same colleague stories about the way our son is very literal and how we have to be careful about the way we word things because he will interpret them at face value. (We once used the "Because I said so" parental phrase for the reason why he couldn't go outside. He promptly said, "SO" and headed outside. If saying the word "so" was the key to going out or staying in, then...) I have also told him about how we have to be very clear and make certain that our words, face, and body all express the same message or our son will be confused by the overall message conveyed. My colleague shook his head and said, "Wow, I have listened to the way you argue over the last year. And it just dawned on me. You practice this every single day with your son, and you don't even know it. What a blessing. You have trained yourselves to dissect a statement in order to make sure that it is very clear and concise, you have trained yourselves to make sure the entire message is clear in your posture, words, tone, facial expression... everything. You practice this every single day. What a blessing you have."

Titus and his Daddy.

Another evening after school Titus was being his usual persistent self. When he has a question, he needs it answered NOW, and the answer must meet his need or he will not drop it. As bedtime approached, a very busy time with four kiddos, he was still asking the same question that he'd been asking me since the very moment he stepped in the door from school. I don't even remember the question -- there have been ever so many, from "why is the sky blue?" to "how do radio waves work?" -- but I had been putting him off and putting him off by saying "I'll tell you later" or "not now." I just didn't give him an answer that would satisfy him. He asked me yet again and I lost it.

"Titus, you need to get ready for bed NOW!" I said in frustration.

"But Mom, you said you would tell me later," he replied.

"Titus … I DON'T CARE." My voice raised.

Tears immediately filled his eyes and he looked at me as though I had told him the worst news ever.

"Oh Titus, I didn't mean that sweetheart. I am so sorry. I DO care about you." I said softly, drying his tears with my sleeve, "I love you. Momma just means that I don't want to answer your question right now. I am tired. How about tomorrow before you go to school we can look up the answer on the internet?"

"Okay Momma," he said and trotted off to his bed.

After that I decided that I needed a better way of dealing with the constant barrage of questions from him. From then on, when he asked Aaron or I a question that we couldn't answer or didn't have the time to answer, we would say something like, "We'll talk about it at 7 pm," or "Can I answer that tomorrow after you eat breakfast?," or if we completely wanted to delay the answer we would say, "can we talk about that on Dec 14th, 2009?" As long as we gave him a time or a date when his question would be answered, he would be satisfied, but as he has a calendar in his head, he will be bugging one of us on Dec 14th 2009, and many other future dates. Our other three children have also become well versed in this style of communicating with their brother, as it makes our life a bit more peaceful.

Because Titus is so literal, we have to be very careful about the programs he watches on TV. One evening, we were watching our favorite Christmas movie, *A Christmas Story*. We'd reached the part where Ralphie has been in a fight at school and is waiting for his dad to get home. Little brother Randy says, "Dad's gonna kill Ralphie!" Titus jumped up: "Oh no! Is Ralphie's Dad REALLY going to kill him? We shouldn't watch this movie any more!" Even children's programs can portray characters that are whiny or throwing tantrums. If Titus sees these he might try out the behavior at school to see what would happen.

70

Likewise, if we watch AFV on TV and someone gets hurt on a video, we, of course, all laugh. But during Titus's day someone would get hurt, he would laugh and get in trouble. He couldn't understand why it was okay to laugh when people got hurt on TV but not when people got hurt in real life. When characters express anxiety on TV, Titus would express his anxiety that way as well.

Talking to Titus about spiritual things can be especially challenging. He knows that the Bible says that we need to ask Jesus to "come into our hearts" so that we can be with him forever.

"If Jesus is going to come into my heart, how does He get in there?"

"How can I hear God's voice?"

He literally embraces the idea that you can ask God ANYTHING. "Hey God, can you help me find the TV remote?"

He understands that when he dies and goes to heaven, he will no longer have autism. When Titus was in sixth grade, we were conversing in the car after a particularly bad day. Titus told me, "I won't have autism in heaven right? I want to die." It was truly heartbreaking and scary for me to think that he had such thoughts at such a young age. He sees dying as the ultimate cure for autism. In heaven he won't have to worry about being allergic to anything, and all his questions will be answered there. He and Aaron have a deal that he will not talk about dying until the year 2050. So far, Titus has kept his promise.

Noah started Kindergarten the same year Titus started second grade. I had a lot of emotions that day. My green-eyed little man was ready to conquer the wonderful world of kindergarten, and I knew he would love every single minute of it. I had the familiar sadness of letting another one step out into the world, but also in that moment I grieved deeply about Titus. I grieved the fact that he was not the boy he could have been. I wondered what might have been. What should his normal second grade year be like? One morning a few months later I was finishing up a volunteer art literacy program in Noah's classroom. As Noah and I were leaving to head home to eat lunch with Dad and the other two, one of the teachers asked me to come look in on Titus as he was having another bad day. I settled Noah outside the door of the classroom with a book, and as I walked in to see Titus, his bright red tear-stained face told me he'd been crying for some time. He was screaming and pulling his hair in the middle of a typical meltdown. At that time he rarely had a meltdown at home, and I'd never seen one this bad. He didn't even notice as I stepped into his safe space. I tapped him on the shoulder and said his name quietly. He looked around, saw my face, and like turning the page in a book, I could see his panic turn to relief. He started calming down little by little; his snuffles slowly lessened as he chose a nearby book. At that point, I needed to leave to get home for lunch. Titus looked at me with those mesmerizing blue eyes. "Momma has to go home to feed everybody lunch now. You have a good rest of your day, okay?"

I gathered Noah and we walked to the car. He took my hand and said, "Are you okay Momma?" Hard as I try I can't usually hide tears from Noah.

"Yep, Momma's okay. I'm just sad that Titus is sad."

Seeing my other three children grow and develop into happy little people was a joy to my heart. But it also caused questions about Titus and his future. Would he be happy? Would he be loved? Would he have the capacity to love? Would he be alone? These are questions that every parent asks about their children, but when your child has a disability, it's amplified a notch or two. These are questions that have no answers. For me the answer is to go back to trusting God along the way. It's okay to wonder, but not to worry. Enjoy the joyful moments in the journey. Sometimes it's an uphill climb, sometimes one can let go and coast. Because of Jesus, and my sweet husband and other three children who needed me, I never hit a "pit of despair." On the bad days I always thought to myself, my son has it much harder than me.

Titus and Noah

CHAPTER 7

Ms. Frizzle and Buddy the Beagle

The summer before third grade was relaxing and fun for our family. We visited The Children's Museum and the zoo in Portland, and did a father-son camping excursion on the Pacific Coast. Titus also got to experience his first few sleepovers with his best friend. The season was especially fun for my husband and Titus. They got the opportunity to go to overnight church camp for the first time. We made sure that Titus went along with plenty of sunscreen and a bright yellow hat which helped Dad keep track of his son a little more easily: all he had to look for was the bobbing bright yellow head.

Aaron: Fun... really fun... camp was a great idea... loved it. Titus' favorite time, sitting by the creek eating Skittles. Seriously, and it was the one time I didn't have the camera and wished I did. He was the picture perfect shot of "not a care in the world." We wandered down to the creek for free time just after buying 2 packs of Skittles at the candy cabin. I had my backpack stuffed with towels, shorts, sunscreen, all of the items an otherwise careless father should have for any mistake that might occur... anyhow, I asked if he wanted to get in. A moderate shake of the head was all I got. So, I slipped into the stream to splash other kiddos as they floated by. I looked over to check on the little guy and he was leaned back against my pack, hat half over his brow, Skittles in one hand while the other fed him morsel after morsel. The world was whirling around him but he was so content. Later I asked him what his favorite part of camp was, he said, "the creek." I asked," your favorite part of the creek was..." and he said, "eating skittles." The simple things.

Titus at camp eating Skittles

I usually felt (feel) uncomfortable with groups of women. Few people "got it." I felt uncomfortable sharing my heart and my day to day experiences. I didn't want to be pitied if I got enough courage to share things like stories of how my son smeared poop on the bathroom walls at school. I really didn't want to hear "I know how you feel." Yet that summer I met two women who would become lifelong friends. God brought these relationships just at the time I really needed good friends who were willing to support me with their prayers and listening ears. I met Jen at a birthday party and later on I got to know her through a Bible Study at my house that we affectionately named Mocha Mammas. Jen is the type of friend who anticipates the needs of others. She would drop by just to check on me. We had many meaningful conversations over coffee and cheesecake, she was always there to listen to what was going on in our house. Most importantly, she and her family invested time in getting to know us. I met Rachel one morning as we were both waiting for our daughters to be released from morning kindergarten. This lovely woman with a darling little toddler approached me, "Don't you live in my neighborhood? I am looking for a walking partner and wondered if you might be interested." Of course I said yes; I was looking for a walking buddy as well, but more so I longed for relationship. We walked a lot of miles together that year in the early mornings and developed a treasured friendship.

As these new friends came into my life, and we got to know each others' families over the next few weeks and months, we found that they were families that were willing to take part in our life and the role autism played in it. They were willing to establish relationship with our little family even though we were quite different than a lot of other families. As time went by, they understood us better and better and really "got it." These were friends I could vent to and call if I had a very difficult day. We cried together on more than one occasion. Because we had no family close by, the DuPonts and the Loefflers became our family. I am so thankful. I am thankful that I have deep enough relationships to cry over when we have to move far, far away from each other.

Rachel: The Haslems are the very best sort of neighbors. They are available, and present, and real and you can count on them. They are the people you call when you need someone to stay with your kids while your husband takes you to the ER. Or the friends you immediately dial when your toddler brings you the phone because you threw your back out - neighbors so gracious they cover your embarrassment at having to (literally) be helped off the floor. During our five years of living right 'round the corner, we had to call on the Haslems for aid several times. And when they had emergencies of their own arise, their own trips to the ER or to car accident scenes, they reciprocated and called us. They invited us to care for their precious children, and we valued their trust.

Then there are the other, less emergent, "every day" kinds of ways we experienced true community with the Haslems. We've definitely borrowed the proverbial "cup of sugar" from one another. (For Karen and I, it was usually the quarter yard of fabric to complete a pressing sewing project). Karen and I also went walking in the brisk early mornings for many months together. Our kids rode bikes, and climbed trees (the Haslems have a whopper of a tree in their side yard in Oregon), and had Pixar movie marathons. Goodness! We even used their lawn mower for one entire Spring! We were those kinds of neighbors.

And when you're neighbors like that, you get to see each other in pajamas, or all dressed up for a much anticipated dinner date. You help each other potty train the babies, and you pass along hand-me-downs. You celebrate Seahawk wins and share birthdays. Actually -- you become more like family than neighbors.

When you are family, you learn to recognize and appreciate some of the unique qualities that each individual family member possesses. As I write, I take a moment to glance up at four dear faces framed in a place of honor above the fireplace. These pictures are among my favorites ever taken of my children. EVER. I am convinced that the reason I cherish them so much is that they were captured by Karen. Karen KNOWS my children, and she found ways to interact with each of them to bring out their own distinct personalities.

The Haslem kids have their own beautiful uniqueness, as well. Titus is inquisitive and questioning. Lots and lots of questions. And you have to keep an eye on that boy, because he will try things again and again, as though to test whether he will achieve the same outcome each time. I am so grateful that the Haslems taught us to understand this tendency through the lens of autism. He is a precious boy, that Titus!

Then there's Noah, strong and caring and sensitive. He's aptly named, given his love for animals. Plus he shares my husband's birthday, so that's pretty special! Ciciely loves cats and purple and sock monkeys, and is such a good friend to my daughter Tessa that I could almost cry. Then there's Lucas. Those chocolate brown eyes and blond hair… they make me melt. Watch out world, because I'm pretty sure the twinkle in Luc's eyes mean he's going somewhere! Yet, what I love most about these three is their compassion for others. They see, really see people, and reach out to them. Perhaps having a brother with special needs has given them this tender sensitivity to others. I am so thankful we've had the joy of walking for a season with this family.

While we can no longer skip on over to share a cozy cup of coffee (or nibble of dark chocolate), there is a tie that binds our hearts together. I'm so thankful God forged our friendship, because the Haslems really are the very best sort of ~~neighbors~~ family.

As fall arrived Titus was excited once again to start school. But despite his excitement, from the morning of day one he had a difficult time. During his first week, he displayed behaviors that were an attempt to gain some kind of control in his chaotic world. His behaviors included peeing in the "safe space" several times, taking his clothes off, hitting and kicking staff and other students, and knocking computer monitors on the floor. His new teacher was a very good teacher and his students loved him. His classroom was decorated brightly with amazing and colorful kites hanging from the ceiling. For most students, this was a calm, fun environment to learn in. For Titus, who hated the wind and the chaotic nature of kites, they were a huge distraction. For a time the staff had to make him a little cardboard barricade along the top of his desk to try to cut down on the distraction. At home Aaron and I came up with a positive reinforcement plan to try to encourage our son to behave appropriately. I made up about 30 little cards that said "Titus had a GREAT day." We asked the staff to hand them out at the end of a Great Day. A great day meant that he didn't display any specified behaviors. The reward of the little cards seemed to help him focus on what not to do and his inappropriate behaviors lessoned. Part of his actions may have stemmed from missing his best friend, who had moved away just weeks before school started. We wondered sometimes how much Titus really enjoyed relationships. His reaction to his friend being gone was a tell tale sign that relationships really were important to him, even though he couldn't verbalize it. This was a reassuring quality to discover, even though it seemed to be painful for him.

Titus and Bodey

At this time in his life, Titus loved the PBS program *Magic School Bus*. It's a wonderfully creative program where the main teacher, Ms. Frizzle, takes her class on educational field trips in a magic bus which transports them through time and space. Everyone loves Ms. Frizzle and her genuine love of learning. Ms. Frizzle has an engaging personality and bright red hair. Titus's teacher that year happened also to have, you guessed it, bright red hair. So of course Titus made the connection and started calling his male teacher "Ms. Frizzle."

"Can you please ask him to stop calling me 'Ms. Frizzle'?" was his request at the first parent-teacher conference.

I wasn't sure he was serious, and I giggled as I replied, "Oh, well, I can try. You have to know how much he likes you... for him to call you Ms. Frizzle. You should take it as a compliment." I tried to sound encouraging.

How do you explain to your autistic son that it's not polite to call your teacher "Ms. Frizzle"? It's not easy. He had made the connection, he loved Ms. Frizzle, he really liked his red-haired teacher: How is it wrong? We tried to get him to stop using the beloved name in reference to his teacher, but because he didn't really understand why it wasn't a good thing, he continued the practice, much to the dismay of his teacher.

As Titus started third grade, Noah started second grade, and our daughter, Ciciley, started kindergarten. This was one of the first times we saw the impact that Titus was having on the lives of his siblings. At various times of the year, counselors visited the different classes to talk about important issues such as how to make friends, how to handle conflicts, and how to deal with a bully. One morning as I was waiting to gather Ciciley from her class, the school counselor approached me.

"I have to tell you what your son said in class today," she said, smiling.

"Oh boy, what did Titus say this time," I asked, wondering at her smile.

She laughed, "No, not that son, I'm talking about Noah. I have to tell you what he said in class today, it just warmed my heart. I was talking to the students today about making new friends. About what if there was a child on the playground who was all by himself. What do you think you could do?"

She smiled at me, "Noah raised his hand right away and said. 'Maybe he has autism and likes to play by himself.' I've never heard that answer before and I was so proud of him for suggesting that. We went on to have a little discussion about it."

"Thank you so much for telling me." My little green-eyed man was very wise.

Ciciley's Kindergarten teacher, Mrs. Hudock, pulled me aside later that same week.

"I have to tell you how wonderful your daughter is. We have a little boy in class this year who is physically disabled and has to use a special walker. The other kids in the class are afraid of him, but your daughter walked right up to him on the first day and gave him a high five. It was like she didn't even notice he was different. Today she noticed that his walker was stuck in the mud on the playground and she hurried over to help him get it out." She smiled warmly. Even now, Ciciley has a deep compassion for people in general, but especially those who have a disability. Our daughter is truly stunning in her outward appearance, but she is even more beautiful on the inside.

We were so proud of both of the kids, but their reactions in these situations demonstrated how much of a positive impact Titus was having on our family. Since our other three children have grown up living with someone with disability, they don't see a boundary between "normal" people and those who happen to have a disability. There is no fear associated with a disability. In fact, all three of our other kids are naturally drawn to people with a disability, and can spot someone with autism like a professional. I don't think they would've developed this gift any other way than by God providing them Titus as a big brother. It will be interesting to see how God uses their experiences as they grow into adulthood.

The year as a whole was really difficult for Titus, and I had a really difficult time watching Titus struggle so hard almost every day. School was not at all fun for him and he would come home utterly exhausted. He was at a point where his environment was so overwhelming, learning was not happening and he could not function. During the Christmas break, Aaron and I decided that it would be better for him to be homeschooled with me for half days for the remainder of the year. The staff was not too happy about our decision. I had been called in to the school yet again to collect Titus during a meltdown and took the opportunity to tell one particular member of the staff.

She looked at me in shock as I was buttoning the coat of my red-faced son, "You can't do that. It's a team decision. We all need to decide what's best for him."

"Yes, I can. I am his mother and I get to decide what's best for him. I don't need to have a meeting to decide if this is a good plan. We're starting homeschool half days, beginning tomorrow." I walked away, taking Titus gently by the hand. It was one of those moments where the Mama Bear inside of me came out again. This was one of many times where people around us questioned our decision, but sometimes as parents, knowing our children better than anyone, we have to gather our courage and go against the grain of what others believe is best. I've learned through the years to make changes if things weren't working in the school system. Sometimes this means taking your child out of his or her comfort zone; though it can cause short term stress, it usually turns out well in the long run.

Homeschooling turned out to be just what our young man needed. We would start out the day in the regular fashion: making breakfast for everyone, then dropping Noah and Ciciley off at school, and Lucas at his nearby preschool. Just Titus and I would read, or bake special cookies just for him, pop over to the library, or work on math worksheets or flashcards. I used a timer throughout the morning and rewarded his efforts and good behavior with Skittles. I made sticker charts that he would adorn with smiley faces. Spending time with him one to one was so nice, but the best part was that we actually started having conversations, something that I wasn't sure would ever happen. We chatted about little things: the latest Pixar movie, why he liked to cook, how great pizza is. It was good to see him relaxed and having fun. Things also began to improve at school little by little. We all decided it would be a good idea for Titus to have a job to do at school, something that would make him feel important and needed. So he began a daily routine of walking from classroom to classroom collecting all the paper in the recycle bins. At home he was in charge of emptying all the garbages. He loved having a "job" and was very good at his responsibilities. His new job allowed him to grow socially as he interacted with different people across different settings.

About a month into our homeschool routine, Titus started talking about building a time machine, probably because we had recently watched the movie *Back To the Future*. I wrote it off, finding it imaginative of course, but no more than that. He talked about it for days. I finally asked him why he wanted to build a time machine.

He said, "I want to go back to 2006 and fix it."

"What do you want to fix?" I said.

He replied, "Because I want to go back to 2006 and behave."

"Maybe it would be easier for you to apologize to Ms. Watters instead of making a time machine," I managed to say, after I almost fell over.

He was really serious now about this whole matter and I could see it. He looked right at me and said, "Mom, tomorrow can I go see Ms. Watters?"

"Great -- let's go see her after school tomorrow," I replied happily, knowing that he was excited.

The following day I was waiting for him in the usual pick-up spot. He ran to greet me and said, "Mom, now can we go and see Ms. Watters?"

We practically ran there with little brother Lucas in tow. When we arrived at her door he was disappointed to find that someone else was in her class and that we would have to wait. As soon as she was available he ran toward her and looked at me.

I looked at her and said, "Ms. Watters, Titus has something to....."

I didn't even finish my sentence before the words came tumbling out of his heart.

"Ms. Watters.. I am <u>so</u>, <u>so</u> sorry for having so many bad days in second grade."

As the words came out of his mouth tears came to my eyes, and her eyes, and I think I even saw a tear in my son's eye too.

"Oh, Titus!" Ms. Watters replied with an astonished look on her face.

She gave him a big hug and said, "I am so happy to hear you say that. And I am so happy that you are doing better."

He looked at her with a big smile. A smile of contentment. The past was made right in his heart. It was a moment I will not forget. In that moment my questions about whether he'd ever be able to express his feelings, or care about someone else's feelings, were answered.

Wanting to build a time machine wasn't the only thing his imagination was working on overtime. He was very interested in the human body and wanted to learn all about it. His favorite book at the time was a picture book called *My Human Body*. Almost every day for months, he would come home and page through it with ferocity. He came to me one day with a request.

"I want to see my bones," was his request along with a sweet smile.

"Oh, well to see your bones you have to have a special machine called an X-ray," I replied, thinking quickly ahead to the next question that would certainly come.

"Can we go to Fred Meyer's and get one? Today?" he said excitedly.

"Ummm... no, we can't. We can't just go buy an X-ray machine, they are very expensive. But they have them at the hospital and sometimes doctors have them in their offices."

"Can we go to the hospital then?" He was getting a bit impatient with me, apparently super mom, not being able to solve his conundrum.

"No, Titus. A person has to be hurt or really sick to go to the hospital for an X-ray. We can't just walk in and tell the doctors that you want to see your bones," I replied.

He was truly disappointed. I ended up finding a little animated movie online that satisfied his curiosity over the issue. But not for long: The next morning before school he came to me, thermometer in hand, and said, "Mom, I am REALLY sick. I need to go to the hospital for an X-ray."

Titus at a tulip farm near our home in Oregon.

On Easter weekend of that year we happened upon a most unexpected blessing. Aaron and I had been talking about the possibility of getting a family dog. A beagle was what we had in mind, since we'd heard they were great family dogs. We had been putting it off in the business of life until one morning Noah and I decided to go to look at the puppies at a nearby shopping mall while we were on our mother-son outing. His eyes were almost as sad as the little beagle puppy in his arms when I told him there was no way that we could spend $750 for a new puppy. We went home and he told Daddy all about his adventure and the "cutest dog in the world." My husband always manages to find a way to please his kids and wasn't about to disappoint. As soon as we left the room he began a search for a beagle puppy on Craigslist. He found one in particular that looked interesting: TWO FREE BEAGLES, THIS WEEKEND ONLY, MUST COME GET THEM. The address was listed there and he quickly wrote it down, picked up his keys and said,

"Let's go for a ride everyone." We also brought along our close friend Cody who happened to be at the house, as his wife was out of town and he wasn't doing anything better that day. On the 45 minute trip to see the dogs, we warned the kids,

> "This does not mean we are bringing home a dog today. We are going to LOOK at them. We are JUST LOOKING, don't get your hopes up." This statement was repeated several times along the way.

As we neared the house, we only had to listen for the sounds of baying beagles to know we were at the right address. Aaron and I and Cody got out first, leaving the kids in the car. The sights and smells before us were very sad indeed. Crammed inside an 8 x 8 outdoor wire kennel were two beagles, barking excitedly. There was no grass under their feet, only a disgusting mix of feces and mud. The only shelter they had was a small dirty white igloo with torn, muddy blankets for a bed. There was not a scrap of food in the dog dish and no clean water to be found. The kind woman there told the story. Her friend was the owner of the dogs and had gone on vacation and had asked her to please find a home for the beagles, as she now only wanted her two new poodles who lived a life of comfort inside the house. Aaron and I took a good look at the dogs. The female had cream and light brown patches and a wagging tail, starved for attention. The male had the familiar beagle markings in black, brown, and cream. Both dogs were overweight from lack of exercise and extremely dirty; covered in bits of mud topped with a thin layer of oil. The most horrifying part was that both of them had bark collars on which were obviously not working, but the little females collar had been on so long that it had embedded itself into her neck. We checked them over looking for any deformities, broken bones, or fleas. Our four anxious children were still waiting in the car while Aaron and I stepped back and talked it over.

"We can't not take them. We can't leave them here, the poor things. If anything, we can find them a home with someone else," I said anxiously. Aaron agreed, still shaking his head in disgust as he took in the scene.

Noah: You can't forget the talk with us after the talk.

"Now, are you guys ready to take care of them?" asked my dad.

"Yes!" said the four of us at the same time, Titus a little late, probably staring off at someone else's yard.

"Now, that means you have to feed them and water them. Are you ready for that?" asked my dad. We all replied in the same way as before.

"And that also means cleaning up their dog poo. Are you alright with that?" asked my dad, but this time, it took a second to think that one over a bit. I think it was Ciciley who said "yes" first. The rest of us answered one at a time.

"Um... yea." I believe was Titus' comment. After that, Mom and Dad went back in front of the van and talked about it a little more. Now, one thing I don't remember was Cody being there. But, then again, I was only, what, eight or something, so I probably wouldn't remember it. But, yea, everything else that's said here I remember.

We loaded the filthy animals into the back of our minivan much to the delight of our four giggling, clapping children. As we made the trek home our friend Cody sat nearest the dogs and kept them calm with his soft voice and gentle pets. When we arrived home, we carefully unloaded the dogs from the car and carried them through the house to the back yard. It was a most delightful scene as the dogs took one sniff of the lush green grass and off they ran. They ran and ran chasing each other in circles around that yard. They acted as though they had discovered heaven on earth. Noah and Ciciley found some old Tupperware bowls and filled them with clean water for our new guests who promptly lapped it all up. Taking all of it in, Titus jumped up and down with excitement and his new friend Buddy gently licked his hand in appreciation. We bathed the dogs carefully in our upstairs bathtub that evening and everyone went to bed with a smile on their face.

Over the next week, we decided that we only wanted and needed one of the dogs. Lucy, the female, was the more dominant dog and also the loudest. Therefore we decided to keep Buddy who was the quieter, less rambunctious of the two, as he rarely barked. We found Lucy a wonderful home with a lady who, when she saw the little girl dog, cried tears of joy. As the kids showered Buddy with the love and attention he must have longed for, we had no idea how much impact the friendly little beagle would have on our Titus.

CHAPTER 8

Bubble Gum and the Key Bank

Over the summer, Titus and Buddy became best friends. Everyone was attached to our new dog but Titus was especially enamored of him. Many times I would find them curled up somewhere, Titus using Buddy as a pillow, reading to the lovable dog. He would tell jokes to the dog too, who of course would happily listen to anything Titus had to say. The connection was a solid one because Buddy the dog didn't expect anything from our quirky 9-year-old. Titus didn't have to say the right words or figure out how to act "appropriately" around the dog; he could just relax and be who he was. When he returned to school in the fall he had an amazing first week. The teachers asked us what type of therapy we did with him over the summer. Our response: "We got a dog."

Titus with Buddy.

Just as I was hand chosen to be Titus' mom, Aaron was hand chosen to be a daddy to our son. Aaron has a special bond with Titus. We had no choice but to bottle feed our first baby and that meant Aaron got to take the 2 a.m. feedings. Late nights between father and son created very special moments. That bond remained intact between an 11 year old who often screamed at his daddy, and a Daddy who had to be the one to deal out the discipline. He is the one Titus listens to the most, but also the one Titus fights against the most. Aaron is able to communicate with Titus differently from anyone else, and the understanding between them is amazing to see. But in those hard moments, I must admit it's painful to watch the struggles they experience-- painful for me and for our other three children as well. During screaming fits, while Aaron was dealing with Titus, I would gather the other children and go outside or put on some music that would drown out the screams of their brother. When these episodes started occurring on a more frequent basis, we decided that it was really important to provide some fun times for Dad and Titus especially to enjoy together. Meanwhile, I could focus on having a great time with the other three and take a little respite from my oldest son's needs. That summer Titus and Dad got to go to church camp for the second time.

Aaron: First, the camp had a new feature this year, a 30 or 40 foot long water slide! The first afternoon, Ti and I went to the candy cabin and then went and watched the other kids going down the slide, followed by a short visit to the creek for some shallow water wading. But the next afternoon, Ti told me he wanted to go to the Snack Shack and then the waterslide. I asked him if he wanted to watch the kids again or ride the slide? He told me he wanted to ride the slide. So we sat and watched the other kids while he ate his candy and got him ready for the event. (This is the first time that he has ever gone down a water slide.) I figured the little guy would make a run down the slide, realize the shock and surprise of the cold water and the wet pool at the bottom and then decide to go somewhere else. Boy was I wrong. He spent the rest of the afternoon running up the hill to get in line so he could go for another ride down the blue monster. Very cool milestone. He did really well standing in line and waiting his turn, only now and then he had to get out of line to come and tell me what he was going to do next, "Dad! Next time I'm going to go down on my knees!" (Which really didn't work well but, it was a grand thing for him to actually come over and tell me this.)

Bad event, I asked another counselor to watch Titus at dinner time while I ran into the kitchen to make him some "safe" rice spaghetti to go along with the spaghetti everyone else was eating. The counselor seemed to get it and said he would keep an eye on him. When I got back to the table with a plate of spaghetti, the counselor smiled and said he made sure Titus didn't get any spaghetti but, he did give him a piece of garlic bread to tide him over. CRAP! (For those of you who don't know, Titus is on a gluten/casein free diet. No wheat, no dairy, and any of their derivatives) Yep, Garlic Bread is chock full of butter (dairy) and wheat flour. CRAP! This meant that the evening would be "loopy" and the morning would really suck for him. And … they did. Plus, the next morning I told another counselor, no pancakes but he can eat the sausage. So the counselor made sure he didn't get any sausage. DOUBLE CRAP! (yep, I mouthed the words at church camp, I am in big trouble now) Sometimes the dairy takes a little while to work its magic. Wednesday night during worship … the room was dry and hot, the kids were jumping around and singing… and Titus was bent over the chair in front of him working that butter right back out the way it came in. By the time I got him out of the auditorium and into a bathroom, breakfast, lunch, dinner, breakfast, lunch and dinner again, all made their way back up, out, and onto the floor. Poor guy. He looked back at me a little later and said, "I shouldn't have eaten the garlic bread and pancake huh? They made me sick..." Yep little buddy, thems made you sick. But he recovered well and the staff was incredible. All 5 puddles were cleaned up before I had Titus cleaned up and into a new shirt. Good job folks.

One of the worship songs had the lines: I am free to run...(kids echo I am free to run) I am free to dance...(echo) I am free to live for you...(echo) I AM FREE! (ECHO) My son had me crying tears of laughter as he exclaimed as loud as he could, I don't want to run, I WANT TO GO HOME! I don't want to dance, I WANT TO GO HOME!.... As the final lines crescendo in repetitive "I AM Free!" repeated 4 times... Titus crescendoed with I WANT TO GO HOME! The cool part was, he knew he was making a joke and smiled the whole time he was doing it.

Titus on the water slide at camp.

Fourth grade was really an exceptional year for Titus in school. Early in the year we decided to ease back into a full schedule by starting him 2 hours later than his peers for the first month. Just that small amount of time spent quietly at home with Mom seemed to add a level of peace to his day. He had a much easier time calming himself down when things were difficult. But one day in class he decided he was finished working on his current worksheet, and defiantly ripped it up and ate it. The stomach ache he got later caused him not to eat his homework again, but the ripping happened several times over the course of the year during meltdowns. Oddly to him, the assignments that he had ripped up would mysteriously reappear in his homework folder the following day. Eventually he gave up on ripping up his work, knowing he would eventually have to finish it.

He also had some interesting adventures outside. After a particularly drenching Oregon rainfall, Ciciley and Titus went outside to check out the damage in the yard. At the bottom of our big yellow slide a large, appealing puddle of mud had developed. Ciciley saw the puddle and giggled, "Oooo.. it looks like chocolate milk!" Titus quickly ran into the house, grabbed a twisty straw and proceeded to try the "chocolate milk," much to the disgust of his little sister. A few weeks later, after watching the movie *How To Eat Fried Worms*, Titus decided to sneak out to the back yard and see how worms really tasted. Apparently they taste better if you wash off the dirt first.

We decided that it would be a good time to explain autism to the kids, namely Noah and Ciciley. They were both old enough to understand and were starting to get some questions from friends and stares from other people. They took it all in stride and knew their brother was different, but I felt I needed to give them some facts to go with the word they'd heard so often. I gathered some children's books together to help me explain the biology of it all and even had a few notes ready. Early one Saturday morning I sat them down in a pile of bean bags and did my little presentation. I read through the books and told them all about Titus' particular case and explained how Titus was a gift to our family from God and we are so blessed to be a part of his life. When I finished, I asked if they had any questions. Noah raised his hand. "Yes, I have a question. Can we go outside now?" As they ran outside, I was reminded again of how gracious a God we serve. The kids were in no way concerned with what autism was. They loved their brother. At that point autism was just a word that adults used in conversations. Telling them that Titus had autism did not change their view of him or their feelings towards him. As they've grown, we've had other conversations about how to deal with Titus when specific issues come up.

We had a similar conversation with Titus as well. We told him about autism and tried to explain it using very simple terms.

"Your brain is so cool!"

"Your brain can do things other people's brains can't do."

"You have autism, your brain is different."

"You are really amazing, Titus!"

We really wanted to help him understand that his difference was just that -- different, not less than. He didn't really understand it all but he knew the term now and we could use the word in conversations and he knew that autism was why he was different. Little by little he's grown to understand the whys behind the physiology. One of the difficult parts about high-functioning autism is that Titus can understand enough to realize that he's different. But the heart breaking part as a parent is not being able to explain why in a way that he will understand. Hopefully someday he'll understand the whys that bother him on the difficult days.

We made an effort to try to help others understand autism as well. We gave the books we had gathered to the school to put in Titus' classroom and eventually into the library for any of the kids to read. We made ourselves available to chat with parents who were new to autism and all that comes with it. God put us on this road for a reason. Aaron and I feel blessed that we have our faith in God and each other to help us in our journey, but there are so many people who do not. I know that many deal with their child's disability as a single parent. Honestly, being a parent to a child with a disability can be a lonely, isolated place to be -- even if you happen to have a loving, supportive spouse. I can only imagine what life is like for single parents with kids on the spectrum. The daily struggles of life can be mentally and physically exhausting, let alone dealing with continual crises and just keeping a household together. I would encourage any single parent to seek out help, even if you feel there's no time to do such a thing. Seek out family members or friends if they're willing to help out, or check with local and state agencies which are set up to help parents affected by autism. Look for parent support groups in your area or even online. I've listed some such places in the reference section at the back of this book. The most helpful thing for Aaron and me has been to talk with other parents who have kids on the spectrum. We've found such hope and encouragement from people who know what our life is like. Seek out people who have been in your shoes.

For various reasons, in November of that year, we made the decision to move Noah and Ciciley to a smaller school in the district. Gales Creek school, the highest rated school in the district, was tucked away in the Oregon landscape just a 20 minute drive from our house. It was a wonderfully small school where the kids were well cared for and well educated. They both made a smooth adjustment and thrived in the close knit school. Titus was doing quite well where he was, and he would be changing schools the following year to an upper elementary school for fifth and sixth graders.

Titus' imagination continued to grow and during fourth grade, it was fixed on one particular issue for quite a while. Ever since Titus saw a particular scene in *Toy Story*, he's been enthralled with claw machines. Our local grocery store, Fred Meyer, had a great big claw machine near the entrance. It only took one quarter and the delight of trying to capture a prize and he was hooked. Every time Aaron or I even mentioned going to the store, Titus would stop whatever he was doing and come running, hoping that we would be shopping at Fred Meyer so that he could come along with a quarter in his pocket. Apparently we just didn't shop there enough and he came up with an elaborate plan to visit the store whenever he wanted. As we were driving by a Key Bank location one day his big plan was revealed.

"A KEY BANK Dad!" Titus yelled from the back seat of our van. "Can we go there?"

"Why do you need to go the bank, Titus?" I said, in expectation of an imaginative response.

"That's where they keep all the keys, right? I need a key to Fred Meyer so that I can open the door and play the claw machine whenever I want!" His response was ever so sincere and innocent. So he was quite upset when we drove right by the place with all the keys, as we attempted to explain that the bank held money, not keys. Not too satisfied with our answer, for weeks afterward he would mention his plan over and over again. Then he came up with another idea.

"When you go shopping, can you please get me two packs of Bubble Gum, please Mom," excitedly waving the wrinkled dollar bill in front of my face.

"Okay Titus, are you sure you need two? I don't want you to eat it all at one time again."

"Oh yes! I have to eat it all in one day. Then I can blow a really, really big bubble. Then I can get into the bubble and float all the way to Key Bank and get the key I need." He was jumping up and down with excitement, sure that his new plan would work.

"Ummm... that is a really great idea, Titus, but I'm not sure it will work. You might get gum in your hair. Do you want sticky gum in your hair?" Excitement left his face as he pictured the prospect of a hair cut.

Early that spring we decided to try looking for another church to call home. Our regular, rather large church was 40 minutes away; we were not getting there as often as we would like and the kids were not meeting kids they would see in school. We decided to try to find a place that was a better fit. Being in kids' ministry for years, Aaron and I have always looked at churches in terms of how the kids are being served. If the kids are well served and growing in their relationship with Jesus, then we felt the rest would fall into place. Our first concern has always had to be, will they be able and willing to serve Titus.

We decided to visit a new church for a Sunday night service. After seeing the other three happily dropped off at their respective classrooms, we took Titus to his assigned room. We should have caught a clue when we signed Titus in.

"Titus. That's an interesting name. How did you come up with it?"

Okay... this IS a church setting, a Bible-believing church, in the kids' ministry department. "Umm … Titus is a book in the Bible. In the New Testament? After the book of Timothy? We named him after his Grandpa Tim."

"Oh wow, really? I never knew there was a book named Titus," he quickly finished writing Titus' name on a tag. "Guess I'm in the right place to learn that."

As we walked into the classroom, we mentioned the facts: Titus has autism and he's allergic to wheat and dairy. The response from the nice gentleman at the door was, "No problem, I know all about autism. My friend's kid has it," and "No big deal." On returning, we were greeted back at Titus' room with "Oh, by the way, he got a donut hole. It was just a little one though." Honestly, we've come to expect that kind of experience in a new place. It's frustrating having to retrain the people who think they know enough. Needless to say, we didn't return to that church. I've often thought life with Titus would be easier if people could see his disability. Blindness you can see, people who are deaf speak with their hands, individuals with Down's Syndrome have recognizable features. People approach Titus all the time thinking he's a typical child, and it takes a few minutes of being around him to know something is different. Some people see our son have a meltdown and at times they must be thinking what a spoiled child that is, or what a brat, or what terrible parenting. People often react with confusion. Titus just wants to be treated like a normal guy. If people could "see" his disability, they might be a bit more understanding.

During this time we were a bit worried about the fact that he still loved toys that were not at all age appropriate. Most 11 year olds are into building models or robots, collecting various items, using MP3 players. Titus still loved Veggietales, play dough, and preschool age TV shows. None of these are bad things: it just makes gift giving a challenge at times. Every time we come to his birthday or Christmas we enter a wonderland, wondering what in the world he would like this time. One year we bought him a remote control car thinking he'd love it. I think he looked at it once and had more fun with the play dough in his stocking. Another year we bought him a case of shaving cream to play with in the shower - he loved it. I think this was the first year that he actually wrote a letter to Santa Claus. What was on the list? A time machine, a claw machine, gumballs, and a *Toy Story* book. Santa was so happy that Titus finally wrote him a list, he got every item on it.

Titus discovered another favorite television program called *Martha Speaks*. The main character is a dog who, after eating alphabet soup, is able to speak English. Not only is the delightful dog learning how to speak English, but also the more subtle aspects of the language. Martha the dog learns about things like sarcasm, figures of speech, homophones, and definitions of various words. Titus learned right along with Martha. The program has been so instrumental in helping him understand the use of language. He started saying things like, "Oh Dad, you're being sarcastic, aren't you?"

Titus finished the year and we anticipated a new school with trepidation. In our school district, five early elementary schools fed into one large upper elementary. As the end of the year approached, the staff took special care and time to take Titus on visits to his new school. Of course all the other kids got to visit too, but Titus went more than once and had his own private tour. Every aspect of the school that he would encounter was checked out in a relaxed atmosphere. At the time, we feared that his wonderful aide would not be allowed to move up with him since she knew him so well. In fact, his aide was not allowed to move up, but as an answer to prayer, his new aide was a perfect match for him. Despite this, the next two years would be some of his most difficult ever.

CHAPTER 9

Raging Hormones and the Missing Eyebrow

"Titus, could you please pass me the bacon," I said one Sunday morning at brunch. Suddenly two pieces of bacon flew across Ciciley's plate and landed next to my plate.

"Thanks Titus... but next time hand me the plate of bacon," I said above the giggles around the table.

"But Mom, you said to 'pass the bacon' so I did!" was his reply, with a giggle and a big smile.

"Okay... you're right. I did. Next time I'll ask you to hand Mom the plate."

Titus was and is so literal. Over the years there have been many times where he sends us all into spontaneous laughter.

Titus had reached an interesting stage in his life. He was 11 and wanting to be more independent, of course. He had this way he liked to argue: he wanted to argue until he won, or thought he won.

For instance, he'd say something like, "Sugar free gumballs are healthy."

"No, Titus, they're not."

"But they're sugar free!"

"Just because it says sugar free doesn't mean it's healthy."

"But sugar free gumballs are healthy -- right Mom?"

"No, Titus, they're not."

"Mom... just say 'sugar free gumballs are healthy'!" He would be crying at this point.

"No, Titus, that's not true." I usually ended such a conversation not by agreeing but by trying to diffuse him, saying "Whatever you say,

Titus." Otherwise it would go on and on and he would get more and more upset. It didn't really matter at that point what we were talking about -- gum or dinosaurs or a movie he's not allowed to watch. It was a pretty typical conversation in those days.

Like most, our eleven-year-old boy was stinky. For a few days I walked around the house wondering what that horrible smell was. I was not ready for my first born to hit puberty, but it turns out that many kids on the spectrum start puberty early. I was so not excited about that knowledge and I certainly was not prepared emotionally. Aaron had a little chat with Titus about showering every day and gave him a quick demonstration of deodorant. At first, applying deodorant was really difficult for him; it was cold, felt uncomfortable, and it tickled to apply it. Eventually he got used to the idea. But for several months he wouldn't wear deodorant on the weekends, "because I don't have to go to school on the weekends." After months of being reminded that "you stink even on the weekends," he eventually gave in and thankfully started wearing it every day. Personal hygiene has never been his best subject. At eleven, he really wanted to grow his hair long "cause I like the way it looks." We told him he could grow it long IF he kept it clean. It has taken him years to tolerate shampooing his hair really well, keeping it clean enough to grow out a bit.

That summer we made a trip back to Montana to celebrate the wedding of one of my nephews. It was a memorable time spent with family. Not only did we get to spend time with my family, but Aaron's parents met us there as well. They enjoyed seeing the grandkids they barely knew and decided to take them all out for ice cream. On their return we heard that Titus tried to run away from them and Noah was able to stop him. "He's fast and sneaky," is what Grandpa Tim had to say about his oldest grandson. On the night of the rehearsal dinner as we all gathered back at the hotel, Titus was suddenly gone. By this time we knew our son's tricks quite well. Most everyone else was starting to panic, but Aaron took one look at the elevator buttons and took a ride up, stopping on each floor until he found his son. Five minutes later, Titus and Dad walked hand in hand down the hall having a conversation about telling others where you are going if you leave.

One Friday evening we decided to have Ciciley's best friend Tessa over for our traditional pizza and movie night, followed by a sleepover once again. Tessa was used to being around everyone in our family, from Mr. Haslem who teased her endlessly to Titus and his quirkiness - she didn't seem to mind a bit. The girls got all the giggles out and went to sleep. After getting up the next morning, they slowly made their way down to the sofa and popped in an American Girl movie. All of a sudden who comes running down the stairs but Titus... wearing nothing but a smile. Talk about a rude awakening. Ciciley was not too surprised, and Tessa giggled, as both girls covered their eyes. Life in our house was so not normal but she loved it anyhow.

On another morning, Titus came out of the bathroom with an interesting look of accomplishment. As I walked closer, I thought something was different about his face. What was it? Then I saw it, or rather didn't see it. Titus was missing an eyebrow. While he was in the shower, he had decided to try out Dad's razor, first on his arm, then on his face. It was all I could do to stifle my giggles.

"Titus, how was your shower?"

"Oh, umm, it was great." He stumbled over his words, seeing the look of suspicion on my face.

"Um, Titus, what happened to your face? It looks different somehow."

"Oh yeah, I used Dad's razor, but just a little bit," he said with a sly smile, hoping to charm his mama. "See," he pointed proudly to the spot where his eyebrow used to be.

"Titus! You should never use a razor near your eyes. Razors are sharp. I am so glad that you didn't cut yourself. You are not allowed to use Dad's razor."

"Oh, okay. I won't use it any more." As I finished our little chat I turned around and quickly found a towel so I could conceal my laughter.

Titus started in his new school that fall. We visited once again just before school started, meeting his new aide and the special education supervisor. Everyone was excited to start the new year off on the right foot.

I don't know how many calls I received that year. Enough to know that I dreaded hearing the phone ring. Several times that year and the following year, I would plan to sneak in some much needed "me" time, a haircut or fabric shopping, and the phone would ring. I would have to interrupt my plan, go to the school and gather my son, who was usually red-faced and emotionally drained. One day was particularly bad. The staff had again set up a special safe space for Titus to have meltdowns in. This one was conveniently squeezed into a utility closet. On this particular day Titus was in such a state that he banged his head against the floor tiles so hard that they cracked. He then proceeded to pull up the remaining floor tiles and break every single one as he threw them against the walls.

Friends would sometimes ask how I kept my sanity. For me it was really important that I had time to do something other than take care of everyone else. I took up the art of quilting when I was pregnant with Ciciley. Even though I didn't have the time with 3 preschoolers, I made the time. The dishes sat in the sink, and the laundry went undone for a while longer. Being able to create something beautiful while engaging my mind was very helpful. I have spent many hours at my quilting machine over the years and eventually I turned my creative outlet into a small business that I operate at home.

Titus and I with my first Autism Awareness quilt.

Titus's bad days were so numerous during fifth and sixth grade. But to this day I still have one saved message that was so needed and so encouraging: "Hi there. I am just calling to say that Titus had a FABULOUS day. He worked hard, he was helpful, he was polite. Really he just had an ideal, perfect day. I just thought it would be nice to get a positive phone call. Let him know that we are very proud of him, and we look forward to a similar day tomorrow."

I don't know how many times I listened to that message just to hear someone praise my son during that difficult season. I was so glad that it was left on an answering machine, so I could listen to it whenever I needed it. The message was a reminder to me of what he was capable of. People who choose to go into the Special Education field are an amazing breed. Like all teachers they work long hours, but at times endure physical abuse and really difficult challenges. Because of this, the burn-out rates in the specialty are high. As parents, we try to encourage all of our kids' teachers, but especially the ones who pour their life into our Titus.

Yet sometimes even these wonderful people had trouble remembering not to expect normal social behavior. For *years* we had been teaching Titus to use declarative language, describing the world around him, and he had gotten quite good at it. One spring afternoon, though, I got a note in the notebook: "Titus told Ms. Z that she was fat. We told him that what he said was inappropriate and asked him to write an apology letter to her. Please talk to him about this issue."

Okay, so how do we explain to our autistic son the social ramifications of telling someone that they're fat? Where is the line between telling the truth and offending someone? This line is hard enough to distinguish for "normal" people. How can we expect our son, who has no social barometer, to understand this concept? A football player might like people to tell him that he's big. A model might like to hear that she's skinny, others might find the word skinny offensive. Titus was not trying to be mean, and to be honest, he was stating a fact. He really had no idea why his statement demanded an apology letter. He was obedient and did write the letter at school. However, he did not get a "talking to" about something we had been teaching him to do for years. I didn't voice my opinion, but my first thought was, 'Isn't this person in Special

Education? She shouldn't be so easily offended by an autistic child's innocent comment." I did try to have him come up with other words besides fat. "How about the word "fluffy" or "chubby" or "round"?

In March of that year, our beloved dog Buddy died. We had found out soon after we rescued him that he wasn't actually 4, as the nice lady had told us; according to the vet who spotted cataracts in his eyes, he was at least 9 or 10 years old. One Friday evening he came inside and seemed to be limping a bit. He was very quiet most of the night, staying away from all of us. After the kids went to bed he curled up in a corner of the room, whimpering in pain. As I opened the door to our back yard he jumped up, yelping in pain, and drug himself to the outside as quickly as he could. It was already dark out and a warm rain was coming down. After we fumbled around trying to find the flashlight, Aaron and I headed outside to check on our companion. There, deep underneath our arborvitae hedges, was Buddy. His breathing was labored and he growled softly as we stroked his head. Aaron and I knew that he was in the last hours of his life. We covered him with a warm blanket and let him be in peace. Aaron slept nearby the sweet dog that night just in case he needed some care. As we woke the next morning, Buddy was barely breathing. We told the kids that Buddy was going to die soon.

"What? Why? How do you know that Buddy is going to die?" Titus was the first to speak.
"Titus, Buddy is an old dog. It's time for him to go to heaven. God wants him to come live with him," I said gently.

We called the vet and made an appointment to have him put down. We didn't want him to suffer and we knew there was nothing the vet could have done. Aaron gently pulled Buddy out from under the hedges and put him on an old flannel shirt. He wrapped the shirt around the treasured dog who had given our little boy so much. We brought the kids out to the back of the van where Buddy lay, still breathing, his eyes open.

"You guys need to say goodbye to Buddy now. Dad will take him to the vet so that he won't hurt so bad any more."

One by one the kids took turns. Lucas, still just a little guy, gently stroked the dog. "Bye- bye Buddy." Tears filled Noah's eyes as he gave the dog one last tummy rub, "Bye Buddy." Ciciley, being the little mom that she was, had a close attachment to the dog. A tear rolled down her cheek as she bent down and gave the sweet beagle a kiss on the head. She choked out one last good-bye and laid her hand on his side. Titus was next. He looked up at me, seemingly puzzled about all the emotions around him.

"Why are you crying, Mama?" Titus asked.

"Oh, Mom is just sad because Buddy is dying. I love Buddy, I will miss him."

"Oh."

"You need to say goodbye to Buddy now," I said quietly, my hand on his shoulder.

"He's going to heaven, right Mom?" he said matter-of-factly.

"Of course he is. God will take good care of him," I said with a little smile.

"Oh GOOD." he said with a big sigh of relief. He bent down and gave Buddy one of his big hugs, and happily stroked the floppy ears. As soon as Titus was done, Buddy breathed his last breath, and died right at that moment with Titus' hand on his head. It was as though he had been waiting to say goodbye to Titus.

"Oh... he just went to heaven. Buddy is dead now," I said.

"Buddy is dead now?" Titus asked.

"Yep, Buddy is dead," I choked out, tears rolling down my face.

"Okay. Dad, when can we get a puppy?" A smile rolled across his face.

The transition from life to death for Titus was very black and white. Life ended. Life goes on. What is next? Later that day we went to the local hardware store and purchased a special stone. We brought it home, let the kids decorate it, and placed it under Buddy's favorite tree.

A couple of months later, we decided to get a puppy. We chose a cute little fluffy Goldendoodle - half poodle, half golden retriever - after researching different breeds that were being used as therapy dogs. Fully trained therapy dogs are very expensive. Originally I wanted to get another rescue dog, but in the end we thought it might be better if the puppy learned how to be around Titus and his quirkiness from the earliest days possible. I took the cute little furball of a puppy, named Kitty Kat, to 6 weeks of training with a local doggie trainer, but with 4 kids and a new puppy, I just didn't have the time to spend with her that was needed. We had hoped that one day she could become a therapy dog for Titus, but he never really bonded with her like he did with Buddy. A high-energy ball of fur was a far cry from the old docile Beagle.

CHAPTER 10

Saturn Gets Crushed and Surgery Fun

I've always been so happy that my son has a sense of humor. Each year that he grew, his sense of humor did too. Around this time we chose to take Titus to a new doctor. He had never seen anyone in this particular office yet, and Titus and I were patiently waiting for the nurse to call him back. The door to the back office opened and out walked a young college-age man who happened to be African American.

Titus looked up at him and smiled and said, "Hi Mr. BROWN!" and then he just giggled.

The young man smiled a big smile, knelt down and said, "Well, hello Mr. WHITE." And then they both laughed. He smiled back at me as he walked out of the office.

That summer Titus qualified for ESY, which is Extended School Year services. He would have especially difficult times in school after a break of any kind, such as Spring Break or Christmas Break. ESY was a way for him to have a session of summer school so that his transition back into the Fall wasn't so difficult. Our school district at the time provided an incredible summer program. It was called CBAP - Community Based Activity Program. The 6-week program was open to kids with disabilities as well as their neurotypical peers. The kids would participate in regular classroom activities as well as many wonderful recreational field trips such as rafting, hiking, swimming, rock climbing, and other fun summer activities. The many volunteers made the program very safe and fun for everyone involved. Titus loved the program. We loved it because he was having a blast and getting to do things that he wouldn't have done otherwise. It was also really nice to have a break from Titus, and I spent some much needed quality time with my other three children. We would go on our own outings where I could relax a bit and not have to be worrying about Titus. Of course, we all loved him, but it was nice for the kids and I to feel closer to normal.

As the school year started for Titus, the staff was prepared with new ideas to help him deal with his anxiety and behavior issues. They used a "How's Your Motor" chart, which sat on his desk, to help him gauge his own levels of behavior. Based on a number rating system, his days would be given a number, 10 being the best, 1 being the worst. It was a very visual way for him to see what behaviors meant a "great" day and which behaviors justified a bad day. The goal here was to help Titus, over time, learn how to calm himself down as opposed to having to go to a safe space to collect himself. This is called emotional regulation. It took years for him to get to the point where he was able to calm himself. Everyone has been so proud to watch him reach this goal over the years.

Many of the behaviors he displayed in the previous year continued. I believe that the onset of puberty sent his body into a tailspin for a couple of difficult years. Like any normal sixth grader, he was seeking independence and control in an environment that was very challenging for him. I would get calls, at times on a weekly or daily basis, from the special education director, telling me of instances of screaming, hitting, scratching, headbutting, and kicking other students and staff. The mom in me was pulled in two different directions. Being the mom of Titus, I was of course concerned about him and his behavior and his safety. Being the mom of 3 neurotypical children, I was concerned about the children who had been in the wake of Titus's frustrations. Most of the time I didn't hear the name of the child or children who took the impact of my son's behaviors, but I was heartsick at the thought of another child having to go home and tell their mama about the experience of bearing the brunt of Titus's anxiety. I prayed for those children and the conversations that would be happening around a dinner table in another neighborhood. I felt helpless most of the time, having to deal with the heartache of my own son's inner struggle. I had to hand it over to God and ask that He comfort those kids. I really wanted to find out who they were so I could pop over and give them a hug and try to explain. Over the years in that quaint community, many people got to know Titus. I can't remember a time when my son wasn't treated with kindness and understanding. Titus, at his best, is a sweet, kind, charming young man. These amazing qualities outweigh the times when he struggles, and people tend to remember the young man behind the behavior.

Titus discovered a wondrous invention called the Vending Machine. Such machines would take your money and give people food whenever they desired. Our son couldn't resist them and would take any opportunity to try to visit them. Titus had such an infatuation with them that he started taking other people's money when he had the chance: loose change from atop a dresser or out of someone else's piggy bank. He would show up to school with a handful of change and head directly to the machine. Thankfully the people with him on a daily basis were smart enough to call me and ask if he was allowed to spend it all at the vending machine. In most of these cases I didn't even know he had taken money to school. When I asked him where he got the money he usually told me the truth: "I took it from Dad's coat pocket," or "I got it from Ciciley's piggy bank." At this point we told Titus to please *ask for permission* before he takes things that aren't his.

The next week the same thing happened and we were puzzled. "Titus, did you ask for permission to take the $5?"
"Yes, I did ask for permission," he said innocently.
"And what did we say when you asked for the $5 bill?"
"You said 'No.' But I did ask," he said with a smile.
At this point we realized that he had indeed *asked* for permission. "Titus, next time you need to ask for permission and the person has to *give* you permission to take their money."
"Oh, okay Dad. I'll do that next time."

The staff also tried a new visual schedule to help keep him on track, calling it the red and green schedule. On his green schedule he was having a great day, red meant he was having a difficult day but could work towards getting back to the green schedule. At this point in his life, just like any other kid, he wanted to be "normal." He wanted *desperately* to be okay and have great days. During one instance at school he was on the red schedule and struggling to "get back to green." He pleaded with DeAna, his aide at the time, "I am okay, I am okay! LOOK AT ME!

I AM OKAY!" He tried to smile really big, while tears of frustration were running down his face.

DeAna: Every day with Titus was the unexpected. I never knew what was going to happen, good or bad. He taught me that no one fits into the mold that's in the textbooks. It's so much deeper than that. He taught me to look deeper, to look behind the disability.

On one particularly hard day, Titus was still very upset after I had brought him home from school. When he had episodes at school and needed to calm down I usually sent him to his room so he could scream in his own space. On this day he had screamed for about 10 minutes, and I decided to check on him as he was quieting down. As I pushed open the door to his room, I found him sitting on the floor against the door. I looked down to see blood smeared all over both of his arms and hands. He had bitten and scratched himself to the point of drawing blood. I took him gently by the hand and led him into the bathroom. I washed his wounds carefully and dried the tears from his red face as his quiet sobbing subsided. I applied some medicine and bandages to his physical hurts, but my heart ached to think that I could not possibly fix the hurt he felt inside. I know every parent faces this issue, but here is a child who really couldn't express his feelings in words; it was extremely difficult to see him express them in the only ways he knew how. Somehow hurting himself was his attempt to fix what was wrong. As Aaron looked at him when he arrived home, Titus said, "See Dad, see," pointing to the bandages scattered up and down his arms, "I *did* hurt myself." No parent likes to hear those words. This was one of those moments where I would have to choose a room in the house, close the door, and just go cry. That was all I could do, cry tears of heartache and pray to The One who made my son. I prayed that God again would give me the strength and wisdom to get through just today.

In October of that year I received a call that no wife likes to get.

"Hi there, are you on your way home?" I answered, seeing that it was my husband calling.

"Um… yeah. Do you know that school on Hwy 199?" Aaron sounded a bit odd.

"Oh, yes, I remember where it's at. What's up? Are you okay?" I replied.

"I need you to come get me. The paramedic here says I need to go to the ER."

"What? Are you okay? What happened?" I begged him to tell me.

"I kinda got in an accident, a guy decided to turn right in front of me into the school parking lot. I'm okay but my car isn't."

"I'll be right there."

I hung up the phone, my heart and mind racing. I called my friend Rachel from down the street. "I'll be right there," she said without hesitation. I quietly told Noah and Ciciley, who had been in the room listening, that Dad had gotten in a car accident; he was okay but he needed a ride home. I purposely did not tell Titus, since he was not in the room when I took the call. I decided that he didn't need to know; the knowledge would've brought about anxiety in him that I didn't want my friend Rachel to have to deal with. It was just better that he not know until he saw his daddy.

I called up the stairs to him in as calm a voice as I could muster, "Titus, Ms. Rachel is coming over for a little while. Mama has to run an errand."

"Okay Mom," he replied, blissfully unaware of where I was headed. As she ran in the house, I ran out.

I prayed all the way as I drove 15 minutes to the scene of the accident. From about 2 miles away, I could see the flashing lights of two firetrucks and an ambulance leaving the scene. As I drove up, I steadied myself and rolled down the window for the police officer on the scene, "That's my husband." He directed me to park near where Aaron was sitting on a guard rail.

I got out of the car and walked over to him, taking his hands in mine. "Are you okay?"

"Yeah... but I'm a little dazed," he said as an EMT approached.

"He is one lucky man. I'm glad you got a call from him, and not from me." He spoke so kindly. "He looks okay right now, but if I were you I would take him to the ER just to make sure. Have them take some X-Rays and check him out. The fault lies with the other driver so it's not up to you guys to pay the bill."

I took a look at my dazed husband and then at his car, or what was left of it. A tow truck was there and the driver was shoveling pieces of

Aaron's car off the highway. He was *shoveling* my husband's car off the road and Aaron did not have one scratch on him. I was amazed at God's protection as Aaron walked to our van and we drove to the hospital.

Aaron and his crushed Saturn.

We spent a couple of hours in the ER that evening. While Aaron was in X-ray I called his parents and other family and friends, sharing the news and asking them to pray. As his mind started working again, Aaron recalled the accident: At 55 mph he had T-boned a man in a Lincoln Continental as the man attempted to turn directly in front of him. His Saturn had crumpled under the impact of the collision and saved his life. Aaron left the ER with bruising on his chest from the seatbelt, as well as a prescription for pain meds that he would certainly need the next morning. Turns out that his ribs on one side were pushed in considerably and it took a chiropractor to discover it a few days later. The young man in the other vehicle had to be extracted from the car and spent 3 days in the hospital with multiple injuries.

We returned to the house late that night, after all the kids had been put to bed. As we walked in, Rachel looked at Aaron in disbelief. He did not look like he had just been in a head-on collision. To this day I am amazed and thankful that God chose to save Aaron's life that night.

The next morning I shared the event with the kids, telling them how thankful to God we must be because our Daddy was home and safe and sleeping upstairs. Titus really didn't understand what had happened but his questions were practical: "When is Dad going to get another car?" "How is he going to get to work?" and "How are *we* going to pay for a new car for Dad?" With the kids off to school, I was not looking forward to seeing Aaron in pain that morning as he woke up. It seemed like any other morning as he came down the stairs and made his morning coffee. He was very tired, and though the bruising was more severe, he was only slightly sore.

Winter of that year brought our first visit to a Portland Winterhawks game. The Winterhawks are a major junior ice hockey team. We got free tickets from a special community group and a bus ride for all of us to attend in downtown Portland. We got to sit with a group of Titus' friends and their families and enjoyed the experience to the fullest, down to getting overpriced, yet delicious hot dogs and drinks. Once again it was an opportunity for us to enjoy something as a family because Titus was so cool.

Spring was a difficult time of year for Titus, as usual. He became more argumentative at home and at school. He started screaming at students and teachers, even throwing other students' projects in the garbage. He also started sneaking food to school in the pockets of his hooded sweatshirts. On the Monday after Easter he snuck chocolate kisses from his sister's Easter basket into those pockets. After he did this a couple of times, I sewed the pockets on each of his hooded sweatshirts closed. He was not happy that his method had been found out.

That spring we attended a "transition" meeting for Titus. He would be transitioning into junior high in the fall and this was an opportunity to meet more new people who play a role in his education. It was all a bit nerve wracking for me. So many things would be new for him in the fall: new building, new teachers, new bus, new kids, lockers, new feelings that come along with new hormones, new schedules. I think the aspect that scared me the most was the new people making decisions. One gal was there who had never even met my son. I showed her a picture of him. "So sweet," she says. "Yes, he is a handsome boy," I thought to myself, sweet even, but she had no idea what he was capable of. This was another one of those times when I had to give it to God and know that He is in control. Starting junior high is a huge transition for any child and their parents. For a child with autism, it's amplified about 10 fold.

A bright spot in the year was the annual science fair for all sixth graders. Titus is always, always asking questions, so coming up with a question to answer as a project was relatively easy. Titus's question: "Which bubble gum is the stickiest?" The whole family got involved as we tested 10 different bubble gum brands. This meant everyone got to chew bubble gum for a science experiment! Needless to say, Titus was even more popular in our house than usual. Aaron, being an engineer, helped Titus come up with an apparatus to test each chewed piece of gum, gross yes, but fun. I helped Titus make a tri-fold board filled with pictures of his project and the scientific results. He was very excited about the project and proudly displayed it on the day of the Science Fair. Though it was a rough year for him, Titus did make great strides in regulating his behavior and learning how to calm himself down.

Throughout that year, Titus complained more and more about his stomach and lower abdomen hurting. He is usually the last one to mention pain of any sort, so for him to bring it up without being asked was concerning. Trying to get our quirky son to describe pain or tell us where it was had always been a challenge. This time however, he made the statement, "It hurts way inside my pee-pee." I made an appointment with the physician's assistant that he normally saw. The PA discovered that Titus had undescended testicles. At first I was alarmed that this problem had not been found before my son was 11 years old. I was under the impression that this issue is present at birth. But it seems that in some cases not until a young man enters puberty does it become apparent. We were referred to a pediatric urologist who saw Titus within a few weeks. He did in fact need to have surgery to correct the problem, something that makes every parent nervous. We had been through surgeries before, with both Noah and Lucas having to go through tonsillectomies, but this was a bit more complicated.

With the okay from the doctor, we decided to wait until August for Titus to have his surgery so he would be able to attend the CBAP program, and still have time to recover before school started. We gathered Titus very early in the morning on the day of the surgery, trying to explain why he couldn't have anything to eat, "It IS breakfast time, Dad." The staff at the children's hospital were amazing and answered all of our son's interesting questions. The surgery itself took about an hour and a half and then he was wheeled into a recovery area. Titus woke up from the anesthesia with a start, but soon calmed down as Aaron talked to him. We were able to take him home soon after with large, very sticky bandages over two areas on his lower abdomen. He was a good patient and slept most of the time for the next 24 hours. For the next few days we kept him on the couch as much as possible, keeping him occupied with Veggietales videos and Pixar movies. After a week we decided it would be safe to take off the heavy duty bandages, especially since the skin surrounding the bandages was getting red and irritated. After much gentle pulling, the bandages were off. We cleaned the area well and put on other bandages over the adhesive stitches that would soon come off. Titus was very good about leaving the bandages alone all day and all night. The next evening, however, was a different story. We had gotten all the kids successfully tucked in and were downstairs preparing for the next day. I heard Titus head to the bathroom and after a few minutes when I didn't hear him return to bed, I thought I'd better check on him. I headed up the stairs and into the bathroom where he was sitting.

"How are you, Titus, are you feeling okay?" I said as I walked into the bathroom.

He didn't say a word. As I got closer I noticed his hands were red, and there were red splotches on his stomach and legs, and on the white towel on the floor. It took me a second to realize that the red splotches were blood.

"Titus, what are you doing? Where did this blood come from?" I said, trying to be calm.

He pointed to where his bandages used to be. I looked at the gaping holes in his abdomen and realized that he had pulled off the adhesive tape stitches little by little and was poking his fingers down into the holes that were now exposed.

"Aaron, I need you!" I yelled out of the room.

Aaron rushed up the stairs and came into the bathroom. He took one look at his son and shook his head in disbelief.

"Oh Buddy, that doesn't look so good." he said, gently taking his son's hands.

Together we washed the blood from Titus' hands and gently wiped off the red splotches from his tummy. I made an emergency call to the doctor. I spoke with his intern, who helped with the surgery.

"Yes, he pulled out all of the stitches and his fingers have been digging in the openings," I said, trying to sound calm on the phone.

She must have heard my anxiety, "It's okay. Don't worry. There are more stitches deeper inside so he didn't penetrate too far. He does need to come in and get it all cleaned up and re-stitched. As soon as you can get here."

We bundled up our son and Aaron took him to the ER at 10:30 at night. They quickly cleaned him up and stitched him up with even stronger stitches. He didn't bother the stitches again, and we kept a close eye on him until the stitches dissolved.

Chapter 11

The Junior High Boy Who Wanted to Be A Girl

Once again, Titus attended CBAP that summer, this time with Noah and Ciciley, who had an amazing time. There was one hitch on the last day of the program, however, when Titus decided to kick sand in the face of a sweet, unsuspecting little girl. I was very unhappy with my son.

"Titus, that is so mean of you to kick sand in her face. If you want to keep your friends you have to be nice to them. I hope she still wants to be your friend," I said in my mom voice.

"Why wouldn't she want to be my friend? She likes me." He seemed confused.

"Ti, people don't like to have sand kicked in their face. It hurts. You hurt your friend on purpose. I hope she forgives you."

This kind of behavior happened most often during times of change for Titus. He seemed to be anticipating the change that was coming, and somehow acting out towards his friends make the separation easier. I made him write an apology letter and he presented it to her along with a flower the following day at the end of the summer BBQ. As he walked up to her, she folded her arms and turned away from him. I didn't blame the poor thing, and I was actually hoping that she'd give Titus a hard time. He shrugged his shoulders and walked away in search of the food. A few minutes later, the little girl, her pigtails bouncing, came to give Titus a hug of forgiveness.

Later that summer, I opened the door to a bubbly young girl. "Can Titus play?" she said in anticipation of my query.

I was shocked and amazed. My son was 12 years old, and never once had any child come to the door and asked if my Titus could play. It had usually been a request for Noah or Ciciley to play, even a time or two for Lucas. But never once for Titus.

"Well, I have to know your name first before I let you in!" I said with a teasing smile.

She laughed, "Oh yeah, my name is Rachel. I live just down the street, across from the DuPonts. I go to school with Titus. My mom says it's okay."

"Okay, well, let me ask the young man about it."

"Titus," I yelled up the stairs, "Your friend Rachel is here. She wants to know if she can play with you."

The sound of 12-year-old excited feet came from above, and he was immediately at the top of the stairs looking down at me and his hopeful friend. "What? She wants to play with ME? But why?" he said, his eyes wide with disbelief..

"Well, I think Rachel must like spending time with you and she came over to see if you would like to spend more time together."

"But why?" he said, taking a few steps down towards the open door.

At this point, Rachel knew just what to say to convince him: "C'mon, Titus. Come show me your favorite computer game. I'll show you mine too!"

As Titus bounded down the stairs he said, "Okay!"

I couldn't help it. My eyes filled with tears of joy as I watched them hurry over to the computer starting to share moments together. Titus had a friend. I took a moment to call her mother, whom I hadn't met yet, to thank her for allowing her daughter to come over. She shared with me that she was equally thankful. Her own sweet young girl had been bullied at her previous school and was in need of a friend herself. My heart melted as I hung up the phone, and I thanked God for bringing these two crazy kids together. That day was the first of many days they spent hanging out together. Rachel knew how to pull Titus into playing; even if he protested at first, she was usually able to stretch his willingness to engage her.

As the first day of junior high for our son approached, I became more and more apprehensive. Everything would be new for him: new teachers, new aides, new school, constant changes. Most of it stemmed from the fact that his fantastic aide from fifth and sixth grade, who knew him extremely well, wouldn't be moving up with him. I have never understood this concept of not keeping the same assistant with a child as they age. Obviously, sometimes it just doesn't work out for the assistant, but when both parties are willing, we thought it the common sense decision to keep Titus with people who knew him the best. Why not give him one dab of consistency in his crazy world? Some school districts do in fact try to keep an aide with a child as long as possible, but our district had issues with that approach. The knowledge that she wouldn't be moving up with Titus drove me to my knees in prayer, asking God to provide just the right people to surround him that year. God answered my prayer in a big way. Just the right people did surround him that year, one woman in particular who really was the best person for him. At our first meeting, she whispered to me, "I got my running shoes ready."

Titus surprised everyone. His transition to junior high was so smooth. He seemed to thrive on the constant change. If he was uncomfortable in class, he knew he only had to wait a matter of minutes and it would be changing. He loved the hustle and bustle of kids in the hallways, as most everyone recognized him. Throughout the year he had very few behavior issues. On the days he did have difficulty it was short-lived, and he developed great self-calming techniques. It was amazing to stand back and watch him mature so much during that year. The most important aspect was that HE knew how well he was doing and he was very proud of himself. It was refreshing to not get *so many* phone calls from the school telling me of his shortcomings that day. Instead, his communication notebook was filled with how great his days had been. It seemed, though, that when he did have difficulties, his issues were bigger and required more wisdom on our part.

During the previous summer, Titus had started talking about wanting to become a girl. One afternoon after VBS, Titus made a request on the way to the car.

"Hey, Mom... I want God to make me a girl," he stated innocently.

"Why, Titus? God made you a boy for a reason," I said.

"But I wanna grow up to be a mommy and only girls can be moms." He was ever so serious.

"Why?" I asked again. There had to be a reason for his request.

"Because moms are nice and daddys are mean!" he said in a deep, stern voice.

I let the conversation drop at that point, not sure where to take it.

As Titus climbed into the car, Noah looked at me with a little smile and said, "Mom, that was his prayer request today too." I rolled my eyes, we both giggled, and we went on with our day. Sometimes, a lot of the time, we just have to laugh at some of the quirky things Titus says at the most inopportune times. Little did I know that the issue would come up again and again in the coming year.

Now, just because a young man has autism, doesn't mean there is anything wrong with the hormones raging through his body. Proof of this happened in the sixth grade when he reached out and grabbed a young lady on her behind "because I wanted to see what it felt like." Honestly, most every young boy wants to "see what it feels like," but most of them have a social boundary built in that tells them it's not a good idea. Titus does not have this social boundary. It has to be learned over and over, sometimes the hard way. One day when Titus was seen jumping up and down in front of the girls' locker room door, trying to get a peek inside, the staff stepped in and tried to explain to him that it was not appropriate behavior. Titus kept asking "Why?" and stating, "I just want to see what their room looks like." He continued the practice until two things occurred. First, the staff came up with the idea of having one of his girl peers catch him in mid-jump: "Titus! That's gross, don't do that! Girls don't like it when you do that." He didn't try to jump up and see through the window any longer, but for weeks he kept insisting on seeing the girls' locker room. Finally one morning, a staff member, who had made sure all the young ladies were out of the room, gave Titus a tour of the girls' locker room. He scanned the room quickly, checking out every inch.

"See Titus, it's just like the boys' locker room," the staff member stated matter-of-factly.

"No, it's not! I knew it! See, the paint color here is different. The lockers are a different color. The toilets are different too. It's *nothing* like the boys' locker room. I TOLD you it was different," he said adamantly.

After the visit to the much talked about locker room, his curiosity being satisfied, he never mentioned it again.

Though he did struggle with what was socially appropriate and what wasn't, he was developing a keen sense of what is right and wrong. He took it upon himself to start pointing out injustices. One morning in math class as the teacher was speaking, he ran up to her and yelled, "Hey, you can't yell at the students. You're fired!" Once again it was a case of having no social boundary. Loads of kids probably felt this way about a teacher they had; Titus just has no social restraint stopping him from saying what he felt. He repeated this behavior several times over the course of the year, each time eliciting more laughter from the kids in the classroom. After several reprimands, he knew it was wrong, but he appreciated the attention he was getting from his peers. One morning during a PE class, he said he wanted to "kill" a staff member. That night at home, Aaron had a serious talk with him about words and how we use them.

I got a call early one morning soon after, much earlier than usual, so I knew something was up.

"Hello Mrs. Haslem, this is the principal, we need you to come to the school right away and collect your son. There's been an incident at school."

"Okay, can you tell me what happened? Is Titus okay?" I asked, worried that he might have gotten hurt. I had never gotten a call from the principal's office.

"Well, Mrs. Haslem, your son decided to bring a 4" kitchen knife to school with him today. We take this type of behavior very seriously, Mrs. Haslem. When can you come collect your son?" He sounded very serious.

"I'll be there right away," I said.

I ran upstairs to tell Aaron, grabbing my jacket along the way. "Guess what *your* son decided to do today?" I said.

"Oh no, now what?" he said, his head still buried in the pillows.

"Oh, he just decided to bring a knife to school," I said nonchalantly.

"Oh no, really? Are you serious? I wonder what got into that head of his. Do you want me to go with you?" he said, sitting up.

"No," I said, "they wanted me there right away." I ran out to the car and as I pulled out of the driveway, I called my friend Rachel. "Please pray. Titus decided to take a knife to school today." As I made the 5 minute drive to the school, all kinds of thoughts went through my head. Did he really want to hurt someone? I didn't think he was capable of that. He doesn't even know how to use a knife. How did he sneak a knife out of the house? What will happen to him now? Will he be able to stay at school? I said a quick prayer that God would grant me wisdom as I walked through the school doors.

I walked into the main office as the receptionist peered over her glasses. "I'm here to see the principal. My son is Titus…." Before I could finish she pointed to a room behind her, with a look in her eyes, I wasn't sure if it was pity or disdain. At that moment, I felt like the worst parent ever.

I walked into the room where Titus sat, his jacket still on, at a round table. "Hi Titus," I said as I acknowledged the other man in the office, whom I assumed was the principal. A look of bewilderment was on his face as he replied, "Oh, Hi Mom." He seemed a bit dazed, but as I spoke to him his look softened.

"Can you tell me what happened this morning?" I said gently.

"Oh yeah. I just brought a knife to school," he said. Titus had no idea that he had done anything wrong.

At that moment the man in the suit opened the desk drawer and pulled out "the evidence": the knife sealed in a plastic bag. It was like a scene out of a police drama. No wonder my son was looking dazed. I could only imagine what the scene was minutes earlier.

"Your son pulled this knife out of his coat pocket this morning as he got off the bus," he said. "His aide confiscated it right away, and escorted him here," he said, laying the evidence on the table in front of me. I looked at the familiar wooden handle, noticing that Titus had picked the dullest knife in my drawer.

"Titus, can you tell me why you decided to bring a knife to school today?" I said with a serious voice.

"Oh yeah Mom. I had to bring a knife to school because I needed to open my locker," he said.

"Oh, I see. Why did you need a knife to open it?" I asked, a bit relieved.

"Well I don't have a key for my locker yet and I've been asking and asking and no one would help me get a key," he said.

"Oh, okay. So you've been asking for a new locker key and no one helped you, so you decided to bring a knife to try to open it?" I asked.

"Yep. That's right," he said.

"Well, Titus, you should never ever bring a knife to school," I said.

"Why not?" he asked innocently.

"Well, knives can be very dangerous, and someone could've gotten hurt. I know you didn't bring the knife to hurt anyone, but it's against the rules to bring a knife to school," I said. "It makes people really nervous to see a knife at school."

"Oh, okay Mom. I won't do it ever again," he said.

"I'm glad, Titus," I said, smiling at my son.

The man in the room was listening ever so intently to our conversation. "Okay Titus, why don't you go get your backpack." Titus headed through the office and down the hallway.

"You realize that we have to take these matters very seriously, Mrs. Haslem," he said kindly. "I wrote up a report here about it. From what he told you he didn't have any ill intent in mind. I'll make sure that I state that in the report. But I do have to push it through to the district office. It will go in his record," he said.

"Yes, of course I understand," I said. "You all have a lot of kids to keep safe here. I understand the rules." He smiled.

"But can you please make sure he gets the locker key he needs?" I said as sweetly as I could.

"Yes. I'll take it upon myself to make sure that gets done," he said as he shook my hand. I walked out to find Titus sitting in the lobby waiting patiently for me. "C'mon Ti, you get to come home with me today. Let's go find something fun to do."

The most frustrating part about the whole incident was that afterward, the locker still wasn't opened two weeks later, when Aaron made a call, asking if he needed to bring in some cutters to open the locker.

Starting in the second semester of that year, the staff decided to put Titus into the SAW program, Students At Work. This meant that part of his schedule for the day included doing various jobs that were his responsibility. He would do tasks such as dusting off computers,

121

watering plants, and collecting shredded paper. He LOVED having important jobs to do and responded very well to the responsibility.

At this point in his life, like most normal kids, Titus started arguing about consequences he'd been given. If he came home with a message in his communication manuel about something negative in his day, he would usually be given some sort of consequence; no computer time, or no watching the favored movie of the week.

Whatever it was, Titus was incensed, "Who told you! How did you find out?"

"I'm not going to tell you how I found out. You're the one who made the bad decision," was my usual response.

"Tell me who told you!" He would be very upset at me for not telling him who ratted him out. He started ripping out pages from the manual that told of an incident. He also started lying about things that had happened at school. In our house, lying is usually more serious than the behavior one is lying about, and we doled out consequences accordingly, much to Titus' dismay. He didn't understand why it wasn't okay to lie. He just knew he hated getting consequences for his behavior, so if I didn't find out about them or somehow didn't believe what the manual said, he thought he would escape his poor decisions.

One Friday afternoon, knowing that I always read the manual, he had written in his own special request:
Can you please buy me some lipstick for my lips! Titus

The issue had come up once again. It had come up, his idea that he wanted to be a girl, several times at home within the last few months. We really didn't know how to deal with it, so we had tried to push it aside and change the subject. But now that it was being mentioned in school, we knew we needed to get to the bottom of it. That evening, after we had tucked in the other kids, we had a serious conversation with our son about his desire.

"Titus, why do you want to wear lipstick and grow your hair long?"

"Because, I want to be a girl!" he said joyfully.

"Why do you want to be a girl? God made you a boy. You can't change that."

"I don't know, I just want to be a girl." Titus will say 'I don't know' in order to get out of answering a question. He always has some sort of answer. His dad didn't give up. After about a half hour of conversing back and forth, Titus told us the real reason he wanted to be a girl.

"I want to have a baby and only girls can have babies. I want to be a girl." He seemed relieved to have gotten it out. Aaron and I looked at one another, puzzled for a moment.

Titus loved babies. Every time we would see a baby in a store or at church, he would go out of his way to "say hi to the baby." Often times I would have to rush to get to the baby first so he wouldn't touch the baby without the mom's permission. Most of the moms we encountered were flattered and more than understanding. So, it made sense that Titus would want to "have a baby."

For the next half hour, we explained the difference between "giving birth" to a baby, "having," and "caring for" a baby. I told him that giving birth to a baby, for a girl, was very painful and that I had to be in the hospital for a few days. Since Titus hates pain, he winced a bit when I shared that information.

Aaron asked him a simple question, "Titus, do I have babies?"

"No, Dad, that's silly. There's no babies in our house," he answered with a giggle.

"But Titus, you were once a baby. So was Noah. So was Ciciley. And you remember when Lucas was a baby, right? I did have babies. I'm not a girl so the babies didn't come out of my body, but I got to have babies around."

We almost saw a light bulb go on over his head as he made the connections.

"Oh. You had babies Dad?" he looked impressed.

"Yes Titus, I still have babies, but they are all bigger now. Do you still want to be a girl?" asked Aaron.

"OH NO, I don't. I don't want to be a girl any more. I want my wife to give birth to a baby and then I can have one. I do not want to be a girl, no way."

Finally we had gotten to the bottom of his request. It was all so innocent and sweet for him to want to be a girl.

Titus and Ciciley in June of 2012

During the spring of that year, Titus developed a love of computer animation. Of course he had always enjoyed watching computer animated movies, but he was finally able to make his own movie. He and his wonderful aide, Nancy, made up a little movie to follow up the story of Nemo, entitled *Finding Dory*. They spent weeks making up a story, drawing storyboards, choosing music and sound effects, and eventually making the movie. Titus was over-the-top proud of his creation. He wanted to make up invitations for everyone. He begged me to call the local movie theatre to tell them to show his movie. Of course it was only a one minute, 26 second movie, but for him it was so much more. We had a little screening at our house, complete with invitations and popcorn, and lots of our friends took the time to come over and share his accomplishment with us.

That spring we decided to try something new for Titus: competitive sports. Since one of Titus' favorite activities had been running, we decided to try cross country. His brother Noah was interested as well, so we signed them up together onto a youth team sponsored by some local running enthusiasts. The practices were every other day after school and the meets were held once or twice a week in the evenings or on the weekends. Several kids that Titus knew were on the team as well, and I felt he would be safe there, as long as Noah was present to keep an eye on him. The problem with Titus in competitive sports is that he has no motivation to win. He is not competitive on any level. During practices he would only run a little while, and then stop to pet the cute puppy he spotted, or take a break to check out the bathroom. When he became bored during the little team chats, he would resort to checking down his gym shorts and adjusting things - much to the embarrassment of everyone but himself. During the meets, he would be excited to go but not motivated to finish. As others were racing for the finish line, Titus would literally stop and smell the roses by taking little breaks on the park benches that were often scattered along the course. "But Mom, the benches are there for people to sit on." During one meet, a coach was sent to run along with Titus to encourage him to keep on running. Titus is built for running, always has been and he does it quite well *if* he wants to. He has always been proportionately tall, slender, and strong with great stamina. As a three year old he would run and run along the beach, only changing directions at our call. He loves to run, but only on his terms. No matter what anyone said, he took his own sweet time finishing the races. Consequently, he finished last in every race he ran that season. All that being said, *he had fun*. He had fun doing something different. He had fun being with the other kids. He had fun getting to go for a snack after the races. Running was not the fun part, it was something he was supposed to do.

The other kids in the program were more than supportive of our son. At the end of one particular race, Titus was of course the last runner. As he finally came around the bend headed towards the finish line, the rest of the kids encouraged him, "TI -TUS, TI - TUS, TI -TUS..." they chanted as he ran the last 100 meters. He loved the encouragement and would sprint to the line, not even winded. This scene repeated itself a few times over at other meets that followed. Each time, I found myself in tears, basking in the scene of a crowd of people encouraging my son to finish the race. How delightful it was to see his peers embrace him on this level. I hope someday soon Titus gets to run cross country again.

In April of that year we discovered a wonderful movie about the life of Temple Grandin, appropriately titled *Temple Grandin*. It's the true story of a women with autism who is highly successful, but like every person on the spectrum faced her own set of challenges growing up and into her adult life. The portrayal in the movie of what it must be like to have autism is masterful. Titus loved the movie from the first time he saw it, of course, and went through a phase when he watched it on a daily basis. Before this wonderful movie came out, the only reference to autistic people in the movies was Dustin Hoffman's portrayal in *Rain Man*, in my mind a very unrealistic view of life with autism. One of my reasons for writing this book is to give readers a realistic view of what life is like on a day-to-day basis for a family affected by autism. If we can allow people to gain a greater understanding of autism and the people affected by it, everyone benefits.

Chapter 12

Warning: Major Life Change Ahead

Titus' eighth grade year was one of the most challenging for our whole family. Yet it was also a time where we saw the greatest changes as Titus matured, in every way. It was a season where we saw God's hand move on our behalf in such a tangible way, more than any other time in our life.

Aaron had been working with the same company for almost 7 years, and had been looking for a change. Having recently earned his MBA, he was searching for a position that would utilize more of his skills. Over the course of the summer and into the fall, he had applied for several positions around the Portland area, to no avail. At the time, there was a surplus of mechanical engineers in the area. Recently his boss had sent him out to New York to help a partner company design a particular product. One afternoon in early November, he came home from work with a question for me. "What would you think of moving to New York?"

"New York State?" I said, laughing.

"Well, seems the company is looking into the possibility of placing someone permanently into that area to drum up business. I wanted to know if it was even an option that we would consider." Oh my goodness, he was serious.

We had sensed that some big change was coming in our lives. We were not sure what it was, but God had already prepared our hearts in expectation. At the time, we had our eye on a big, beautiful house down the road that would make a gorgeous bed and breakfast. We had been dreaming about that house for ages, even though it was out of our price range. But over the summer it had dropped in price enough that we approached some close friends and asked if we could borrow money for a down payment. Our friends graciously said no, and we took it as a no from God too.

We spent many hours talking and praying about the possibility of a big move to New York. For a small town girl who grew up in Montana, the thought of moving across the country was way out of my comfort zone. However, for my husband, whose family moved from state to state several times during his childhood, the desire to move is in his DNA. Years earlier we had seriously considered a move to New Zealand, but I just couldn't move *that* far away. For me, this decision required some very clear direction from The Lord. I wasn't willing to make the move without it.

I spent several days researching the schools in the Hudson Valley of New York State. Meanwhile, Aaron was sent to New York once again and did some research of his own. One night he was driving around the area after his work day was done, and happened to need a place to turn around. As he pulled to the side of the road into an unknown drive, his headlights flashed on a sign: "Anderson Center for Autism." When he got back to his hotel room that night, he called and told me what had happened. We took it as a first sign from God that we were on the right track, considering this move. At the time, we were unhappy with how our current school district was functioning. The district had decided to close the great little school the kids had attended, and I was homeschooling our younger three children for the second year. Titus was doing rather well in school, but we knew we needed to consider what opportunities would be available to him after high school. Earlier in the fall I'd had a frank conversation with the autism specialist who had gotten to know Titus very well. I told her we were considering buying a house that we could turn into a business so we could possibly employ our son. Her recommendation was that we find a way to employ him if we could, because the opportunities for him in Oregon would be limited after he finished high school.

After two weeks of research and consideration, we decided that in order to make the move, the offer from Aaron's employer, when made, would have to be exceptionally good: it would have to cover all of the moving costs, travel expenses for us to get to New York, and a raise substantial enough to cover both the cost of living increase and the added responsibility that Aaron would be taking on. We did as much research as we could and came up with a number. To us, it seemed like a number the company would have to stretch to match. We figured if they came up with that number, we would take it as a "yes" from The Lord. In the past, annual raises had been shoved aside and bonuses were cut short, so in my mind it felt unreachable; the company would say "no way" and I'd be able to stay in my nice little comfort zone. About a week later they came back with an offer and a number... in fact, the *exact* number that Aaron and I had in mind. Knowing that we had gotten a clear answer, we said yes to The Lord and the biggest move of our lives. Though our number was met, we knew that God was only using Aaron's job as a vehicle to move us out to New York. We felt that our purpose there was more than just a job.

As we came to the decision, we chatted openly about it with our kids. As they had questions, we answered them, not wanting to keep anything from them. We talked about our fears, and the great potential behind the move as well. Everyone was a bit apprehensive about the possibility, except Lucas who thought it was a grand idea, because we would be close to Maine.

Titus had *a lot* of questions:
"Where will I sleep?"
"What about my bed?"
"Where will I go to school?"
"When does the bell ring?"
"When will school end for the day?"
"What about spring break?"
"What will our house look like?"
"What about my teachers and friends here? They will miss me too much."

Lots and lots of questions. We tried to answer each one as simply and understandably as possible. I looked up the schedule of our new school to get the specifics that he needed, and that seemed to help. On one trip out, Aaron took the time to make a little video of the area, the kids' new schools, and our new house. These things really seemed to help Titus and our other children deal with our life changing event. For some questions, we didn't have the answer, yet.

"Titus, I don't know the answer to that question, yet. But when I know the answer, I'll tell you right away."

His biggest concern was "When? When will we move to New York?" As a young man who lives by a calendar, it was his greatest concern. He needed a date, on the calendar, solid. For weeks, we didn't know, and were not able to put a date on the calendar. He reacted with inner frustration that spilled over into behaviors at school. One morning on the way to school, he decided to try to choke himself on the bus with the seatbelt. Though it was highly unlikely that he would've succeeded, we took his behavior seriously as a reaction to the move. Later that week he told his aide, "I'm going to drown myself in the pool on April 17th." That same day, my voice shook as I called his pediatrician, explained the situation, and asked that he be put on a medication we'd previously discussed: an anti-anxiety, anti-depression med that would help him deal with the changes. Over the years, Aaron and I had discussed putting Titus on medication for his behaviors. The conversations always ended with the decision that it would be a last resort option. Yet if ever there was a time that he needed help coping, this was it. His whole world was about to change and he was trying to deal with it on his own. We decided to put him on the lowest dosage possible and see what happened. Within in a couple of weeks he was remarkably calmer and not at all disconnected, a side effect we had feared.

At first, moving to New York state was the last thing I wanted to do, or ever thought I would do. I knew we were supposed to move, but my heart was fearful and I just wanted to stay where I was. But as I prayed and thought about it, God put a genuine excitement in my heart about the changes. The more research I did, the more The Lord confirmed to me that He had great things ahead. From November through February, Aaron was sent to New York every 2 weeks. We used that time to research every aspect of our new life. The first hurdle we faced was finding a school system for the kids. Aaron interviewed the top 3 school districts on our list, in search of the best one in the area. Titus's educational needs were our first measuring stick, but our desire was to find a place that would provide our other three children with great opportunities as well. One district was very friendly, but Titus would be bussed to another location, a good distance away from the community we would live in. District number two was an excellent district with high performing students, but our impression was that Titus would tarnish their image. District number three was perfect. It was rated an exceptional school, had great student to teacher ratios, maintained high expectations of students, and best of all, provided excellent resources for Titus, who would be educated in the local schools. Compared to the resources of our current district in Oregon, it was amazing. We had decided on a place: Red Hook, New York.

The next hurdle was finding a place to live. Aaron was able to do some house hunting: I would find homes online for him to look at, and he would drive by, in some cases meeting with an agent to view the home. We thought we'd found the perfect one, but it fell through when the owner didn't want to make a deal. It was another clear direction for us. After that, we felt renting would be the best option. Aaron found one of only a few suitable houses in the area, and signed a one year lease.

Once we had decided on a place to move to, and a house to move into, we had to decide how to get there, and on a moving date. Titus had calmed down considerably since starting up his meds, but he *really* needed a moving date and the plan laid out for him. Everyone needed the plan.

I had yet another chat with our trusted autism specialist, who had become a friend as well. "What would be the best way for us to get there for Titus? Should we fly or drive?"

"I think it would really be best for him if you could fly, that way the change all happens in one day, not in a matter of days. Don't drag it out. If you can afford to, I would fly."

Since the company was paying for the move, we booked 5 tickets. Aaron would put the kids and me on the plane, and then he would pack the last things from the house into the van, along with the dog, and take off the next morning. We finally had a moving date, April 3rd. Titus was thrilled to have a date on the calendar and immediately stopped asking "when?"

We decided that since we were moving across the country, we needed to spend Christmas with my family in Montana. My dad and Grandma Mardene were overjoyed as we made the 14 hour trek to their home, which was decked out in typical Skogen fashion. It was a bittersweet visit, knowing that I would not be coming back for a long time. As I said goodbye to my Dad, my heart broke. It must have been terribly hard for him to see us off, knowing how very far away we would be moving.

We had an open house the weekend before we moved, with so many of our treasured friends and neighbors. Many of them were teachers and aides who knew Titus quite well. On this day as he said good-bye to many people, again it was black and white. This season in life was ending, another was beginning. He loved seeing all the people but didn't seem at all sad or upset. He was matter-of-fact about the whole deal. The other three kids took it all in stride as well.

Titus and his wonderful aide Nancy.

I was so busy with the ordeal of the move, I didn't really have time to think about the fact that my whole life was about to change, which, in hindsight, was a good thing. Things got even busier as moving day approached. We spent the last week loading up our possessions, in the

132

middle of which, Aaron caught a nasty flu bug. Our last day in Oregon was spent with dear friends. For our last outing in the area we decided to go to the go-cart track and let the kids have some fun. Titus especially loved the go-carts. The chances of him getting a real drivers licence are slim, so he treasures the licence from the go-cart track. As we drove away from our house in Oregon for the last time, the kids sat quietly in the van, favorite possessions in hand, ready for the next adventure.

One of the most unexpected blessings in all of this was finding a new church family. We weren't really looking, thinking that we'd find a new church home when we were all settled in our new house. But once again, God had a better plan. During one of his trips out to New York, Aaron took a weekend to visit some local churches. He visited several, checking out the youth group scene mostly, now that our kids were starting to enter their teen years. He happened upon a particular church on a Sunday evening. The visit turned into the beginning of a delightful unfolding of His plan for our move. There, Aaron had the pleasure of meeting Pastor Malcolm for the first time; they engaged in a conversation that God used to once again confirm our decision to move.

Aaron called me that night from his hotel room, "Guess what! I found a church." He told me all about his evening and his conversation with Pastor Malcolm. Near the end of our moving process, though we hesitated, Aaron sent an email, asking him if he would be willing to pick up the kids and me from the airport in New York City and drive us to our hotel near our new home. In response to our email, he not only committed to picking us up, but also to letting us borrow a vehicle while Aaron drove ours across the country. He and his sweet wife went above and beyond, blessing our family.

Pastor Malcolm: I walked into the Junior High Youth Room to pick up my 12-year-old son. Entering the room the leaders turned and as one voice cried, "That's the guy you want to talk to." Being a pastor at this church, my first thought was, "What did I do that someone's not happy about?"

Aaron came over, introduced himself, and proceeded to inform me of his family's impending move to the area. Getting over my initial shock of folks wanting to move from the Pacific Northwest to the Northeast, Aaron explained that what he was in need of was information about my second son, Josiah, and our experience with the autism services in the area.

We talked at length of the truly outstanding services to be found in the Mid-Hudson Valley when it came to Special Needs services in general, and autism spectrum services in particular. We also spoke about the school districts and their work with autistic children, and what I was most proud to speak about, the way my church had gone to great lengths to not only love my son, but to work with us as parents to both provide services for him at the church level that would enable him to participate fully, and stand with us in instructing and molding Josiah on some of the social behaviors he was needing to work on. As with many families with loved ones on the spectrum, the diagnosis originally received for our son was devastating. Yet, our God was very gracious, having known more of our story than we could have imagined, taking us from a state with very few services before Josiah was even born, to a state (and a rural area at that) with more services for our yet-to-be born child than we could have possibly imagined.

That initial conversation led to a number of emails, online chats, and phone conversations as Aaron, Karen, and the kids prepared for their New York arrival. I had the pleasure of receiving Karen, Titus, Noah, Ciciley, and Lucas at the airport the day they arrived on the East Coast and driving them to their new temporary home. Having spoken with Aaron so much already, I felt like I already knew these strangers coming out of the terminal. Sadly, Titus had developed a cold just before they all left and was very quiet. Having dropped them at their temporary housing, thankfully Titus got better, but the rest of the family became quite ill.

Sunday night Youth Group was coming. I called Karen and asked if Titus and Noah would like to go. Karen said Noah was ready but wasn't sure if Titus would be willing. I assured her that Titus would be cared for and that the youth group leaders were ready to have them both. When I arrived to pick the boys up, the door opened, and I'm not sure Titus even said goodbye, he was already at the elevator bouncing with anticipation to go. We went, had a great night, and I brought the boys back to Karen. She asked how Titus did, and I said he hadn't stopped talking about youth group and going the next week the entire ride home. A weary mom smiled broadly. When the boys went in she said to me that Titus must sense that I could be trusted, since he does not easily go with strangers.

Whatever it was, I knew I had a friend in Titus. Over the next several months we had the joy of knowing the Haslem family, Titus would always *ask when he saw me if I would be picking him up for youth group – and I gladly said yes.*

How do you occupy 4 children on a 5 hour flight? Simple. You pray like crazy and have half the population pray too. I also packed each of their backpacks with favorite snacks and treats, MP3 players, surprise gifts, puzzle books and favorite stuffed animals. Titus in particular carried his Kindle, and Blue Bunny in his backpack and clutched his giant stuffed manatee, Barbara, in his arms. We got some funny but understanding looks as we made our way through security. It's not often you see a 13-year-old boy clutching a stuffed manatee. My own carry on was complete with address book, wipes, snacks, thermometer and meds since Titus, unable to escape the flu bug, had been running a low grade fever for the past 24 hours. We left Aaron on the other side of the security gate and walked down the long hallways to our flight. Having found our gate, I had the kids pick a spot to sit while I approached the gray-haired man at the desk.

"Good morning sir. I need to make a request," I said kindly, hoping for the best. "Our tickets were purchased online by my husband's assistant, and she was unable to get us 5 seats together. It is really imperative that we sit together. You see, this is moving day for my children and I. One of them happens to have autism and it would really upset his day if he didn't know where we all were sitting." The man raised his eyebrows as I spoke but listened to my spiel.

"Let me take a look at those tickets you have, and I'll be working on that for you," he said, peering over his glasses, "You can take a seat over there, and I'll call you up." I smiled, as I handed him the tickets, knowing that God had taken care of this already.

As I sat down, I realized that I really hadn't had time to breathe in the last few months. I had been busy researching, organizing, packing, and cleaning. The day was finally here. Today was the first day of our adventures in New York. My children were oblivious really about what was ahead. But they were peaceful and calm inside. I was especially thankful that my Titus was at peace.

The man at the desk had been calling out names for the last few minutes, and after awhile, he called mine. I took a deep breath and walked up to the desk.

"Okay, I've been working on this special, just for you. You get the very back of the plane, the last row, 5 seats, all to yourself," he smiled up at me.

I was overjoyed, "Oh, thank you so much. You have made my day so much easier."

It couldn't have worked out any better. We were first to board the plane that morning and made our way to the very back of the plane. Tears filled my eyes as I thanked God for his provision. "Mom, are you okay?" Ciciley said with concern, seeing the tears in my eyes. "Oh yes, I'm great. I'm just happy to *finally* be on our way!"

CHAPTER 13

Look Out New York, Here We Come

The kids did remarkably well on the non-stop 5 hour flight from Portland, Oregon to New York City. A really helpful aspect for Titus, especially, was the screen on the back of each seat. These screens displayed a large map of the U.S. which used a little plane icon, showing us what part of the country we were flying over. It gave Titus some vital information: how long we had been flying, exactly where we were at, and an estimate of our arrival time. This saved him from some anxiety and me from answering the age old question, "are we there yet?"

It was a bit surreal, stepping off the plane that afternoon. I put Noah in charge of his older brother, and I took Lucas by the hand with Ciciley next to me. It seemed as though we walked a mile through a maze in JFK. As we entered the baggage claim area, our predetermined meeting spot, Pastor Malcolm had already spotted us as we made our way down the stairwell into the area. I immediately felt at ease as the man with the kind face made his way to our little group. I thought he looked like a former college football player. Noah thought he looked like a big truck driver. However he looked, he was so very nice and led us through the rest of our journey that day. As the kids excitedly peered at the far off Manhattan skyline, I remember being uncomfortable in the traffic of the city, thinking to myself, "how did I ever get here?" Once we made our way into the suburbs I was able to relax. Soon enough we were pulling up to the doors of our hotel. The kids piled out, excited to start their search for the pool -- one of the only requests they had in the planning of our move to New York state.

By the time we were settled in our room, Titus was feeling much better and his fever was gone. That first evening, as the kids were enjoying relaxing in the pool, I was making some phone calls. I remember telling my sister, "I am so looking forward to this week. I am so tired from the move... we are just going to relax and get to know the area a bit. We'll also have a chance to clean the new house before Aaron arrives." The following day I took the kids to the local Barnes & Noble and Target stores since we all needed to visit a familiar place. I picked up some cleaning supplies and craft activities to keep the kids busy that week. We spent another evening at the pool, in anticipation of visiting our new house the next day. The flu bug had other plans: at 2 a.m. the next morning, I awoke to Noah throwing up in the bathroom.

Later the following day, the flu hit me as well. The next four days were the worst possible way to start our life in New York. The cleaning and exploring that I had hoped to accomplish were replaced by spending as much time as I could in bed, in a hotel room, in a place I'd never been before, without my husband. The kids recovered fairly quickly but were stuck in the room with a very sick mom. Aaron was in the midst of his 5 day trip across the country, stopping in Billings, Montana to pick up his sister who helped him make the drive. I was so thankful that she was able to help him; it eased my mind considerably, knowing that he wasn't alone on the long trip. We chatted on the phone two or three times a day, updating each other on our status and reassuring each other that it would all calm down soon. Through all of this chaos, Titus did incredibly well, as did all the kids. He entertained himself with movies he had brought along as well as his Kindle, and his favorite TV channel which had the familiar TV programs on it. Several times that week, Pastor and his wife visited, bringing us meals, since I could barely function. By the time Aaron and his sister arrived, I was still sick but ever so happy that we were all together again.

Aaron: The moment I put my family on the plane I was back in our van and packing up to head out across the country. The trip was nearly 3000 miles and took the better part of 5 days at 10-12 hours of driving each day. The miles and hours were filled with updates on the travels of my family. The plane flight, their arrival at the airport, arrangements with flight agents to get seats close to each other, meeting Pastor Malcolm. And then the not so great updates. Noah, who had not gotten sick in Oregon, now had a fever. And then, Karen had a fever. I sent several texts and pleas for help to the one person I knew over in NY. Pastor Malcolm ran meals and looked after my family in the ways I couldn't. Panera Bread soup runs, outings to Youth Group. But the scariest and yet, funniest call came on a late afternoon.

"Hey there sweetheart, how are you guys doing?"

"Um, well, I can't get the GPS to work. I keep typing in letters … but I can't get it to find the address. There's something wrong with it and it won't stay on the same screen and … we went over to Target and got some cleaning supplies, and we were going to go try and do some cleaning but,… I can't … the GPS isn't working and it isn't making sense."

"Sweetheart … how is your fever, how are you feeling?"

"Well, I still have a fever, and I didn't sleep very well and, … I can't get the GPS to work."

"Sweetheart, I need you to turn off the car, take the keys out, and tell the kids you aren't going anywhere right now. Now, turn the car off and go back inside the hotel and get some sleep."

"Um, ok, that's probably a good idea. Ok, love you … How is the drive going?" "Its going good, now go get some sleep."

Here I was, thousands of miles away, and my wife is delirious from lack of sleep and a spell of the flu. And she was planning on driving over to our new home to try and get some cleaning done. I thank God the GPS wasn't working. There are many times since that we have cursed the GPS for not working and getting us lost but, this was one time I was thankful that it frustrated my wife enough that she gave up on the contraption and went back inside.

The new house was fairly clean by the time our belongings arrived in New York. Pastor Malcolm had kindly organized a group from our new church to help us unload. Aaron had already unloaded the TV and DVD player from our van into Titus' new room to keep his anxiety level down amid the chaos. It was really amazing to see how well he was adjusting to our major life change. As long as he had the plan and the most familiar aspects of his life around him, he was calm. Of course he did have questions, as did all the children, but he didn't seem to be anxious about anything. He was however, really ready to see his new school.

In preparing for our move, I had already been in close contact with our new school district, filling out paperwork and faxing them copies of IEPs and other needed information. Soon after Aaron arrived we all made a visit to the district office to officially sign the kids up for school. It was a daunting process, but the people we met were so kind and helpful to all of us. Being from the West, we had always heard how rude the people on the East Coast were. From the first day we arrived, the people here have been the friendliest we've ever met. Everyone we came in contact with was very friendly and very genuine. I was delightfully surprised that my stereotype of "East Coasters" was shattered.

The Monday after our arrival was the first day of school for the kids. We purposely chose to start them in the new school system in the Spring. First, we wanted the staff at his new school to get to know Titus before he made the transition to high school in the Fall. Also, we wanted our other children to be in school for a little while before summer, so that they would have made some friends before the activities of the warm season began.

While all of the kids made a smooth transition into the school system, it was quite an interesting first week for Titus. Of course the school district had received his IEP and other pertinent information, but not really knowing our son, they chose to put him in all of the regular classes. He was, however, in the care of a one-on-one aide as he went from class to class that first week. After his first day of classes, he came home very happy.

"Guess what Mom? I got to learn algebra today!" he said excitedly.

"Really? That sounds exciting. What else did you do today?" I asked.

"I got to go to science and gym too. It was a great day." A big smile spread across his face.

I was glad to see him enjoying school so much, but I knew his new schedule of classes wouldn't last. So I wasn't surprised when I got a call later in the week asking me to a meeting to discuss Titus' needs. The individuals in attendance at the meeting were so friendly but seemed somewhat confused.

The math specialist spoke up first: "He doesn't seem to be grasping algebra at all. Has he ever had pre-algebra classes?"

Trying not to sound rude, I responded, "You have seen a copy of the IEP I sent from Oregon, right? You do realize that he has autism? I would imagine that it's very difficult for him to grasp algebra, considering he is still working on his multiplication tables."

The science teacher had concerns as well: "Has he ever dissected anything?"

"Umm... does it involve sharp instruments?" I said smiling.

"Yes, it does," she seemed confused.

"Well, then no, he hasn't dissected anything and I wouldn't suggest he do so anytime soon." I was giggling by this time. I was wondering if this was supposed to be a serious meeting.

The school counselor spoke next, trying to gently break the news to me: "I think that Titus belongs in a more specialized atmosphere. He just doesn't seem to fit academically into the regular classes."

"Well, yes, I certainly agree with that. That's where we expected him to be when we moved into the district. There is such a great program here for him. Honestly we were confused at why he was placed in the regular classes at all."

There seemed to be a collective sigh of relief around the table. Most everyone had to leave at that point and the counselor and I continued the meeting. He explained the terrific program that was available to Titus. He took me on a tour of the specialized classroom that was just upstairs from where we held the meeting. The main teacher in the class was very welcoming and explained exactly what Titus would be doing in her class. The focus was on academics as the kids worked towards a transition into high school and ultimately an unmodified high school diploma. A modified diploma is not academically recognized by the state of New York or institutions of higher learning. In the specialized classroom, each student had their own work area, essentially a little cubicle that they could decorate. The classroom also had a central area for group discussions and projects. We liked the fact that the classroom was located in the junior high school where Titus still had the opportunity to socialize with his neurotypical peers. The following week Titus started in the new specialized classroom, much to his delight. He decorated his cubicle with pictures of Martha Speaks characters from his favorite television show. He came home happy every day, seemingly loving every moment.

The transition to our new life in New York was amazingly smooth for Titus. Almost every aspect of his life had changed: new house, new school, new town, new neighbors, new doctors, new stores and restaurants. He seemed to welcome the changes with excitement. I am convinced that it was all due to my Moms In Touch prayer group; together we covered our family in prayer during the months of preparing to move.

Of course the changes were new to all of us. While the kids adjusted to a new school, Aaron was busy at work and I was busy at home getting the house together. Our new neighbors were all so friendly and helpful and the neighborhood was full of kids. It was a beautiful area that we had moved to, but I sincerely missed seeing the snow capped mountains of the West. I also missed my friends being so close. I hated going to the grocery store in our little village and not seeing one person I knew. I'm not sure if it was because of the water in our new area or because of stress, but in the course of a month I lost almost half of my hair. I would brush my hair after a shower and the brush would be full of hair. I suppose it was a blessing that I didn't have time to worry much about it, because it was so upsetting, but eventually the hair loss stopped.

Soon after we had made the move, Titus had a major growth spurt. In the first 6 months we were there, he grew 6 inches and gained 15 pounds. At about the same time, Noah hit a growth spurt, growing about 4 inches. By August of that year both of the older boys were taller than I was. It was very strange for me, after so many years of having "little boys" around, for them to be taller than me seemingly overnight. It made me to sad to think that they were no longer little, and they wouldn't be little again. I enjoy them as young men, of course; it was just another change that I was not really prepared for.

Group hug.

That summer, Titus attended a summer school session for 8 weeks. While it wasn't, unfortunately, anything like CBAP, he loved it. One of the things he learned during summer school was that he would soon be old enough to learn how to drive. With that knowledge, he began to ask the question, "When can I learn how to drive?" We knew the time was coming when we would need to talk to Titus about this sensitive issue. It was going to be one of many conversations we'll have to have that are difficult for him, and heart breaking for us as parents.

"So Mom, when can I learn to drive?" he said anxiously one afternoon.

"Titus, come sit down and we'll talk about it," I said, directing him to sit on the couch. He sat down in anticipation of us making a plan for him to drive.

"Ti, you know you have autism, right?" I started in.

"Of course I do, Mom."

"Well, some people with autism are not able to drive," I said gently.

"What?! Why not?" he said, standing up. "That's not fair."

"Well, people with autism sometimes aren't able to understand the rules of driving. There are lots and lots of rules that you have to remember, and lots of directions you have to follow," I said, trying to be as clear as possible in my answers.

"Why are there lots of rules? That's not a very good idea," Titus said, a bit incensed.

"Titus, lots of people are not able to drive. Not just people with autism. People who are blind cannot drive either. Or sometimes people are too old to drive. There are lots of people who don't drive," I said.

"Well, I *need* to drive. All of my friends will be driving," he said. This was sounding like a conversation with a typical teen.

"Titus, I'm sorry. I don't think you'll be able to drive. But maybe you should ask the doctor about it. Maybe she will have some good advice for you." Our new pediatrician was very well versed in how to deal with autism. She had her own son with autism, who happened to be a few years older than Titus. I knew the conversation about driving was not at an end; it would surely come up again and I needed some ammunition. I also knew that Titus would probably take advice on this subject from the doctor better that he would take it from me.

Late that summer, we made the visit to the pediatrician. As soon as she stepped into the room, Titus fired his question at her.

"Hi Dr. P. How are you today? I want to know when I can learn to drive. My Mom and Dad said I can't. What do you think?" He looked at her expectantly.

"Well, that is a great question, Titus. Let's give you a check-up first and then we'll chat about it." She always treated Titus with the utmost respect and care. She looked at the changes in his height and weight and commented, "Wow, Titus, you sure are growing. I wouldn't be surprised if you grow to be over 6 feet tall. Are you getting good exercise too?"

"Oh, yes, of course I am. But when can I learn how to drive?" he said, unable to wait any longer for her response to his all important question.

"Well, Titus. Your mom is right. Some people with autism are not able to drive. You know I have a son with autism, right? He gets to ride the bus everywhere he goes. He does very well. He is going to college in the fall."

"Really? He is?" Titus said, amazed.

"Yes, he is. Now, how are you getting along on your bike?" she asked.

"Oh, I ride my bike all the time Dr. P.," he said, looking at me as he said it. I shook my head at the doctor. Titus never rode his bike, ever.

"Well, Titus, if you want to learn how to drive, you have to get really, really good at riding your bike first. The same parts of the brain that you use for riding a bike are the same parts that you use for driving a car. So, you need to go home and practice on your bike. Then we'll see how you do."

"Okay!" he jumped up and down excitedly, "I will go home and practice on my bike."

That very afternoon, he asked me to get his bike from the garage. He didn't attempt it for too long, as the rain started to fall near the end of the day. The next day was Saturday and he was up bright and early as usual. As soon as Dad stepped outside, Titus quickly followed. "Dad, can I practice riding my bike today? Dr. P. told me that if I get really, really good on my bike, I can drive!" He bounced down the stairs like a puppy, following his dad.

Aaron got the bike out of the garage and worked in his woodshop as Titus practiced on his bike.

Aaron: Ti's bike is a recumbent style trike. It has a big wheel in front with pedals and two smaller wheels in the back. Its a little bit like the Big

Wheels we used to ride when we were kids. When first considering a bike for Titus we decided that a trike might be easier for him to master. His overall coordination is not the greatest, a trike allows him to focus on controlling the bike without having to worry about maintaining his balance.

One thing to keep in mind as you imagine this lesson in controlling a vehicle, the house we were renting at the time had a very long, steep, s-turn winding, gravel driveway. Not really the best learning environment for riding a bike, but it presented enough of a challenge for Titus while keeping him close and safe. Second, this was supposed to be the first of many "practice" lessons on riding a bike in preparation for learning how to drive a car. In the course of this lesson Titus got his bike stuck twice while trying to power himself up the hilly drive, where in I was summoned to help him get out of and further up the hill. He ran into our van three times, took two bathroom breaks, and one water break.

At the end of a "grueling" 45 minute practice session, Titus jubilantly jumped up from his bike and declared, "Yes! I did it! I can learn to drive a car now!" I giggled. "What Dad? What's so funny?" "Titus, you have only been practicing for 45 minutes. That's not a lot of practicing. And, in the last 45 minutes you got stuck twice and ran into the van 3 times." "No I didn't. I didn't run into the van..... the bike did."

Thus began another lengthy conversation of dissecting words and concepts.

I walked over to Titus and his bike and stared at the bike. "Titus, how does your bike move? If we stand here and stare at it, will it move all by itself?" I prompted the bike to move and get going. "Don't be silly." "How does the bike steer itself around?" "Ugh, it doesn't." "So, your bike only moves when you pedal it, and it only steers when you turn it?" "Yes dad." "So, it may have been your bike that hit the van, but, you are the one that was peddling it and steered it into the van." "You're right dad, I guess I need more practice."

Later that evening we had a chat with Noah, acknowledging that Titus will probably be very jealous of him in a couple of years when he gets to drive. It's another one of those issues we'll have to deal with as it comes.

The most dramatic event of the summer happened one evening in mid-July. Aaron and Noah had just returned from a "Pig and Pistols" event sponsored by our church, a day spent out in the woods shooting at targets, fellowshipping and, of course, eating. They arrived home just in time for dinner and we all sat down to eat. Our dinner conversation had started as usual and I asked Aaron a question. Now, since my husband is a deep thinker, at times it takes him a couple of seconds to answer. I asked again, no response. I looked across the table and he appeared frozen, not even blinking.

"Aaron, are you okay?" I said. No response.

I walked over to him, "Aaron, are you okay? What's wrong?" He barely turned his head and said, "I cnnnnnt tk." His words were slurred together. My mind raced and I went into emergency mode. The first thing I did was pray while we were all still sitting at the table, "Jesus, please be with us, help Mom do the right thing, and keep Dad safe. Amen."

"Noah, find my phone, quick."

"Ciciley, go over to the Wilsons and get their nurse, quick as you can."

Noah handed me the phone and I quickly dialed 911.

"911 Dispatch, what's your emergency?" said a voice.

"Yes, I think my husband is having a stroke," my voice was shaking but calm.

"Okay, tell me what's going on."

"His speech is slurred, and he seems to have lost his ability to move. He is just sitting here at the dinner table."

As I was speaking to the 911 operator, Aaron started to move his arms and legs again, and began speaking a few words. The 911 operator asked me to ask him to smile, and then to stick out his tongue. Aaron did these things, and all appeared normal. Ciciley ran in the door with our neighbor, Mr. Wilson, who happened to know a bit about the hospitals in the area. The nurse, who was usually at their house, had gone home for the night, but he was a much needed voice in the room as we made critical decisions.

After I hung up with the 911 operator I explained to the kids what was happening: "I don't want you all to be afraid. But it looks like Dad has had a stroke. A stroke is something that happens in your brain, but he is not going to die. An ambulance will be here in a few minutes to take dad to the hospital. They need to make sure that he is okay. Mr. Wilson will be here with you until I come back later tonight." Mr. Wilson nodded his head in agreement.

By the time the ambulance arrived, Aaron was up and walking, and talking. After the EMT checked his vitals, he was able to put on his shoes and walk to the ambulance, unassisted. The kids were sitting around the dinner table as this was all happening. Thankfully, Titus remained calm the entire time; he was just watching, and asked a few questions about what the people in uniforms were doing. I quickly grabbed a few things and followed Aaron down to the ambulance. I got in the car and followed the ambulance for the half hour drive to the hospital.

I made several phone calls while I was in the car. The first one was to Pastor Malcolm. "Hi Pastor, this is Karen Haslem. I need you to pray. Aaron just had a stroke." He was shocked, having spent most of the day with Aaron. He asked if there was anything he could do, and told me to keep him posted. My next call was to Aaron's parents, who were not home, then to his sister who promised to give the message to them. Lastly, I called my brother who has prayed with me in the midst of the most difficult moments of my life. He prayed with me again at this moment, while tears rolled down my cheeks.

After an interesting evening at the ER, Aaron was transferred by ambulance to a more specialized hospital in Albany, New York. As he was being transferred, I made my way home to be with the kids. They were all sleeping soundly, and I thanked Mr. Wilson for his kindness in staying. Aaron spent the next 4 days in the hospital while the doctors tried to figure out why an otherwise healthy 39-year-old man would have had a stroke. He had a series of blood tests, a CAT scan, an MRI, and an ultrasound on his heart. On day four, he had a second ultrasound of his heart, taken with an endoscope put down his esophagus. This test revealed that Aaron had a hole in his heart, which was the cause of his stroke. The neurologist in charge of his case recommended that he take an aspirin once a day. A few weeks later during our follow up appointment, the doctor said, "As long as you keep on the aspirin regimen, I shouldn't see you ever again." What wonderful news to hear. Aaron was especially impressed at seeing the MRI of his brain, which proved the fact that he actually was brain damaged.

During the whole ordeal, I felt God's covering over our family. So many people were praying for Aaron and the rest of us. People from our church that we didn't even know dropped by meals for us that week. Since I didn't really feel capable of driving to Albany to visit Aaron, another couple from our church took it upon themselves to drive me up to the hospital on the day he was released and brought us back home again. We were so blessed by the outpouring of love and support during that time. I was so very thankful to God again, for sparing my husband from a life-altering condition. This story could have had a very different ending.

Aaron and Titus one week after the stroke.

CHAPTER 14

Our Young Man Goes to the Prom

"The dumb kids ride the short bus." This was the wisdom the little neighbor boy shared with Lucas one day that fall.

"Oh really? The dumb kids ride the short bus?" I said in response. "Who do you know who rides a short bus?"

"Titus does of course, Mom, every day," his dark brown eyes looking up at me.

"So, is it true what Sid says?" I asked.

"Well, no. That's why I was a little confused. Titus is so smart, Mom. He can do lots of stuff we can't do. You know, like the calendar in his head," he replied earnestly.

"You are right. We know the truth. The truth is that only the really smart, cool kids ride the short bus," I said, kneeling down to his level.

"But why did he say that?" Lucas said, his arms folded across his chest.

"Well, maybe he doesn't know anyone with autism yet. Maybe pretty soon he'll get to know Titus and see how really smart he is," I said.

"Oh yeah, that's a great idea," he said as he headed up the stairs.

Lucas and I on his first day of 3rd grade.

My first thought after the conversation with my 7 year old was, "Who ever told that little one about the kids on the short bus?" How did the neighbor boy get that idea in his head? How sad to think that someone so young already has a preconceived idea of people who are different than he. As much as we like to think that society has changed in the way we view people with disabilities, there will always be those who choose to believe that those of us who have a disability are some how less than everyone else. That mentality is so short-sighted. Think of all the greatness to be done in the world if we choose to embrace those with such amazing minds. Instead of living in denial and fear, I hope we choose to welcome these amazing people, one in 68 children now, into our midst and work with them to make a better world. Our little world is a better place with Titus in it. Challenging, yes, but changed for the better.

Titus was super excited about being in high school. During the IEP meeting at the end of his previous year, there was talk of holding him back. "You know, Titus can stay in the 8th grade again if we feel he's not ready for high school yet," stated one of the gentlemen at the table.

"Well," I said, "You are going to have to break the news to him. He is so looking forward to high school, I think it would break his heart to not be there next year."

His current teacher had her own opinion, "If his transition from Oregon to New York is any indication of his transition from junior high to high school, he won't have any problem moving up."

First day of high school.

Indeed, his transition into high school was amazing. He loved every minute. His classroom was once again integrated into the same building as his neurotypical peers. The classroom was staffed with very well qualified teachers and a group of 6 other amazing kids on the spectrum. It was a close-knit little community. We didn't know how close until the evening of open house. Open house night is where all the parents are invited into the school, their child's schedule in hand, and expected to attend each of those scheduled classes in 10 minute increments. We walked into the specialized classroom where several other parents were already seated.

"Oh look, it's the new family!" was the first comment we heard.

Everyone seated got up and headed towards us with excitement. We were showered with hand shakes and hugs, and introductions such as, "I'm Betty. I'm Brandon's mom. It's so nice to finally meet you. I've heard all about Titus." The reaction to us was totally unexpected, and a bit overwhelming. But we sure felt loved and accepted. As we left the school that night, we had an overwhelming sense that God had indeed sent us to just the right place for our son.

Titus has always been a charmer. Back in Oregon, everyone who spent any time with him really got attached to the young man. When we were contemplating our move to New York, one of my thoughts was, "What if they don't accept him like they have here? What if they don't like him there? What if he doesn't have any friends?" I suppose I forgot for a split second the power of his charm. Evidence of this happened one morning on the bus ride to school. Titus convinced his bus driver that he "had a meeting" with his previous 8th grade teacher at the middle school. The bus driver believed him and consequently dropped him off at the wrong school. Thankfully, the staff there knew Titus and took him to where he needed to be.

Early that spring, as usual, Titus had some behavior issues in class. He seemed to become more easily frustrated and didn't want to follow the directions. At one point he started pushing over chairs and yelled at his teachers and classmates saying, "I wish you all were never born. Then I could do whatever I wanted!" Later that week I took Titus to the doctor and we discussed his behavior. "I can see that he has grown so much but we haven't adjusted his meds to account for that. Let's up his dosage a little and see what happens." In a matter of days, he was back to his old self, happy and compliant, most of the time.

Titus had the opportunity to enjoy a wonderful rite of passage that spring, a high school prom. Each year a local high school in the area puts together a special prom just for kids with disabilities. They send out invitations to all the special education departments at the other high schools in the area. The hosting students do all the decorations, and provide food and refreshments, supervision and aide to those in attendance. It is such a wonderful opportunity for everyone involved.

A month or so before the event Titus and I had a chat about it.

"Hey Titus, are you excited about the prom coming up?" I asked.

"Well, yes, of course I am. Uh, Mom, what is a prom exactly?" he replied.

"Oh, it's so much fun Titus. You will love it. There is music and dancing and food and decorations. It's kinda like a big party with all your friends from school, plus you might even meet some new people." He started jumping up and down when I mentioned food. "Do you think you might want to go?"

"Well, sure I want to go. Will they have food that I can eat there?"

"I'm not sure buddy, but maybe I can make you something special to take with you, just in case." I didn't want a lack of food he can eat stop him from attending the event.

"Okay!" he said, giving me a big thumbs up sign.

"Great! Do you think you might want to take a date to the prom?" I asked.

"Umm... what do you mean a date? The date of the prom is March 28th."

"No, not the kind of date you see on a calendar. Another kind of date is someone you take with you to a special event, like a friend who might like to have fun too," I replied. "Can you think of someone your age who you might like to ask to come with you?"

"No, not really. No, I can't think of anyone," he replied after thinking for a split second.

"Well, what about Liz? Liz loves to spend time with you and you guys have fun when you're together," I suggested.

"Oh yeah, Liz!" he said, jumping up and down.

Liz was a delightful young lady who happened to live in our neighborhood. Our families had spent time with each other and Titus and Liz always got along well. She was one of the kids who was never embarrassed to interact with Titus at school, stopping to give him a hug in the hallway, or say hello at lunch. She was patient enough to hang out with Titus and have conversations. He was very comfortable around her as well and would genuinely laugh and have fun with her.

Before I allowed him to ask her to the prom, I checked with her mom first to make sure that it would be okay. I didn't want Titus to be disappointed or put Liz in the position of not knowing how to react to his request. After I got the okay from her parents we took a little walk to Liz's house.

"Okay Titus, here's what you need to do. When you go on a date with someone, it's important to ask her parents for their permission first."

"Why do I need to do that? They're not going to the prom," he said.

"Yes, I know, but you are a nice young man and nice young men always ask the girls' parents for permission first. Then if they say 'yes,' you can ask Liz."

"Okay Mom. That sounds good," he said as we got to our neighbor's door.

He walked in without ringing the doorbell or knocking, too excited for pleasantries. As soon as he saw mom and dad he said, "Hello there, Mr. and Mrs. Wilson, can Liz go to the prom with me?"

Our friends the Wilsons were used to Titus's quirky ways, "Well, Titus, when is the prom? We need more details."

"Oh, don't you know, it's on March 28th at 7 o'clock p.m. at Arlington High school." I took the opportunity to whisper in his ear, "tell them that your dad will drive, and we'll pick her up at 6:30."

"Oh yeah, my dad will drive us and we'll pick her up at 6:30. Can she go?"

"Yes, Titus she can go." Mrs. Wilson replied.

Titus started jumping up and down with his thumbs up; he was so excited. Liz walked into the room, already aware of the question that was coming.

"Hi there, Liz," he greeted her with a wave. "Would you like to go to the prom with me?"

"Yes, Titus. I would like to go with you to the prom," she replied sweetly, her red hair brushing across her face.

"YES!" More jumping up and down, "She said 'Yes' mom, She said 'Yes'!"

"I heard, that is so great. You guys are going to have a lot of fun," I said. I whispered another tidbit into his ear, "Tell her that you'll need to know the color of her dress when she finds one."

"What? Why? I'm not going to be wearing a dress. Why would I need to know the color?" he said with a shocked look on his face.

"Because you'll want to make sure the pretty flowers you get her will match her dress." I had forgotten to talk to him about this aspect of prom etiquette.

"I'm getting her flowers too?" he asked.

"Yep, flowers too," I said.

"Okay. Flowers too," he said, giving a thumbs up to Liz, who along with her parents had been listening to our etiquette conversation all along.

A couple of weeks later I got to take my son shopping for a suit for the big event. I really knew nothing about shopping for a suit, Titus being my first son. I took him to a local department store where I knew they had a lot of dress clothes for young men. After we had wandered around aimlessly for awhile, a nice young gal approached us and asked if she could help. She helped us find a couple of things among the racks and I sent Titus off to the dressing room. It was like having a very large preschooler trying on clothes.

I stood a little ways from his dressing room after he'd been in there for a few minutes. "How's it fit, Titus?"

"Oh, it fits grrrrreaaatt!" he said happily.

"Okay, well, Mom needs to see it on you, okay?" I replied.

"Oh, okay. Here I come!"

He stepped out of the dressing room, shirt totally untucked, pants hiked up to his chest and one arm out of the jacket. "See, Mom, it fits great!" He wasn't trying to be funny, but he made me laugh.

I giggled, as the gal helping us stepped back patiently. "Yes, I see how it fits." I said as I adjusted the clothes here and there. A smaller size pants and a few minutes later he stepped out again, this time looking a little older already.

"Oh wow, Titus, that looks so handsome on you. Now I think we need to find you some shoes and a nice tie."

I was glad that there wasn't too many people in the store that evening, as we would have gotten some strange looks as my gangly son bounced around the store in his socks, jacket half off, as we searched for some shoes that fit. The young gal that was helping us was ever so helpful. There were no strange looks or comments from her about my son. While Titus was back in the dressing room I took the opportunity to thank her.

"Thank you so much for helping us tonight. You took a lot of time with my son and I really appreciate your patience."

"Oh, it was no problem. I hope your son has a great time at the prom," she replied with a genuine smile. Sometimes as we have "normal" experiences like this, I wonder if we've made an impression on someone. A lot of people hear the word "autism," but many people haven't actually experienced being around someone with autism.

The big day soon arrived and Titus and I were off to pick up the corsage for his date. He was very excited about the evening.

"Are you excited for tonight, Titus?" I asked. "You are really going to have a fun time."

"Of course I'm excited Mom, don't you know?" he said.

"I am excited too. Mom and Dad get to do something special as well. We're going to hang out at the prom for a little while and..."

Startled, he interrupted me in mid-sentence: "What? You're going to be at the prom too? But it's just for kids, you can't go. I think it's against the rules." This was another "normal" conversation with a teen-ager.

"Titus, you didn't let me finish. I was saying Mom and Dad will hang out at the prom for a few minutes to make sure you are settled, and then we're going to a little party for just the parents of the kids in your class," I said calmly.

"Oh, whew," he said, wiping his brow. "I was worried, I really didn't want you to stay."

Titus on Prom night.

Aaron and I helped him get dressed that evening. He didn't look at all awkward as we took pictures of our handsome son on the stairs. He looked so grown up and happy. We took more pictures at Liz's house, of course, and headed off to the prom. As they stepped out of the car, Dad showed Titus how to hold out his arm for Liz, to escort her where ever they would walk that night. They made a cute couple, and we followed them inside. The theme of the prom was Candyland. The music, provided by a DJ, was not too loud. The most popular place of the night was the photo set. Kids were already crowding around it, taking selfies and group pictures. All of the many groups of kids were having a blast. We left after just a few minutes, leaving our cell number with Liz, just in case. We spent the rest of the evening with the other parents at one of their homes. It was so nice to be in good company, and we felt like we were on a date ourselves. Titus had a really fun time at the prom that year but was ready to come home. He usually heads to bed at 8:00 sharp, and we were surprised that he didn't fall asleep in the car that night.

In June of that year, Titus and his classmates put on their annual talent show. This was a first for Titus, never having really performed. He chose to sing for his talent and he chose a song from his favorite movie at the time, *Frozen*. Titus and one of the teachers in the classroom decided to perform together. Unbeknownst to us, Titus had been learning how to dance for months as part of the choreography for his performance. They worked on his costume in class, and asked me to make him a royal cape so he'd look like a handsome king. On the day of the performance he wasn't a bit nervous and stepped out on stage like a pro.

Titus singing at the annual talent show.

158

Now I am one of those moms who has the tissues ready when my kids perform. I'm just a sap for the joy of seeing them in the spotlight. This was really our first opportunity to see our oldest perform. As soon as he stepped on stage, my eyes filled with tears. There was my son, looking so tall and handsome, singing so joyfully, oozing with confidence. When he started dancing, I really lost it, tears rolling down my cheeks. I started to feel embarrassed at my tears, then I remembered all the other parents in the room who were just like me. It's one of those moments that I never even dared to imagine for Titus. As a mom with a special needs child, I had tucked away hopes and dreams that I might have imagined for my son, tucked them away so I wouldn't be heartbroken when he didn't get to do wonderful and amazing things. God had other plans. Titus does get to do amazing and wonderful things, things that bring us great joy and delight, made even sweeter by the struggles he's had to go through to get there. It was a wonderful talent show. Titus was truly amazing, as were the other kids in the class. Everyone celebrated their accomplishments.

One of the last activities of the school year was a birthday party for one of Titus's classmates. All the families were invited to the Saturday event, so we brought all of the kids. It was really fun to see Titus interact with the kids in his class. It all looked quite normal, all the teen-agers at one table having great fun, and all the parents at the other table engaged in great conversation, eating good food. We all enjoyed each other's company and no one batted an eye if one of the kids happened to do or say something inappropriate. We'd experienced it all before. Even to the siblings of the kids, it was all normal. It was refreshing to be in a group without having to explain anything, just to enjoy where we were and the people who were with us. For us the get togethers are a great resource. We were still new to the group, as Titus was the youngest of his classmates. So if we ever had a question about the area, the services available, or any other matters, we would just have to ask, and someone there usually had an answer.

As the gathering ended, the kids got together for a group photo and all the parents took advantage of the moment, pulling out their cameras. As the kids said good-bye, Aaron looked at me and whispered, "Did you see what I saw?"

"No, what did you see?" I said curiously.

"Titus and Danielle... they were holding hands the whole time during that group photo session," he said smiling.

"Oh, really? How did I miss that? That is so sweet." I really was sorry that I missed the moment.

As we started home in the car I couldn't resist: "So, Titus, did you have fun today at the picnic?"

"Of course I did, Mom," he said.

"Really, what was your favorite part?" I said.

"I got to have a hamburger and a hot dog!" he said joyfully.

"Oh, well, did you enjoy seeing your friends?" I said, trying to pry it out of him.

"Of course I did, Mom. You know that," he said.

"Well, did you have fun with Danielle?" I asked, trying to sound innocent.

Silence.

Aaron couldn't hold back any longer. "Titus, did you hold Danielle's hand?"

Silence again. Then, "How did you know I held Danielle's hand?"

"Because I saw you hold her hand. Was that nice?" Aaron said.

"Umm... yeah." Titus said slowly.

"Oh good, I'm glad you held her hand, she is a nice girl," said Aaron.

"You are?" said Titus with relief.

We ended that year by having a big birthday bash for Titus at our house. We decided to do a "movie on the lawn" event, inviting all the kids in Titus's classroom. I even rented a popcorn machine and provided candy bars and soda for the kids, in lieu of a cake. Everyone had a fantastic time, especially Titus.

CHAPTER 15

Have Scooter Will Travel

"Titus, stay with me so I don't get lost," said my brother, who was in charge of keeping track of Titus that fall day. We were all visiting New York City and Uncle Fred wanted to make sure there was no running for his now teenage nephew.

It was really nice to have two sets of extra eyes that day in the city as my brother and his wife were visiting us for the week. Usually, an outing with Titus in the city, or anywhere else unfamiliar, is stressful for me. I have to be on full alert all the time, making sure he is within my sight. Whenever we do go on such an outing, we all wear our neon green Seahawks hats, which stand out very well in a crowd.

Titus with his Uncle Fred in Times Square.

Just before school started that Fall, Titus came up with a brilliant plan to make his life easier. He wanted to go to California to find a new mom. Apparently I wasn't good enough for his needs. I was giving him too many consequences, and I wasn't grocery shopping enough, and I didn't let him "do whatever he wanted." Again, this is a typical teenage response to a mom, but Titus, who is uninhibited by a social boundary, is much more likely to say how he really feels. My feelings were hurt at times, but I was thankful that he was able to express his feelings. Many kids with autism don't get to that point.

He would say things like, "I'm really angry at you," or "I am so sad right now, see I have tears in my eyes." He was able to express his feelings! This is a great step. So although I was a bit sad that he wanted a new mom, I was thankful.

His plan was elaborate. One evening he quietly came down the stairs and announced, "I'm going to fly to California to get a new mom."

By this time, I was used to his making statements that came out of the blue, and wasn't alarmed at all. "Oh really, that's nice Titus," I said calmly. "Why are you going to California to get a new mom? I'm sure there are lots of nice moms right here in New York state."

"Oh but Pixar Animation studios are in California and I decided I want to go there and my new mom will take me there whenever I want to go," he said, jumping up and down in anticipation of such a visit.

"Oh, that sounds like fun. I wish I could go too. But how are you going to get to California?" I said.

"That's no problem Mom, I'm going to fly there on an airplane, of course," he said matter-of-factly.

"Great," I said, "but how are you going to get to the airport?"

"Oh, well, you and Dad can drive me to the airport," he said.

"Well, Titus, Mom and Dad are really busy these days. And I don't think Dad would like the fact that you are going to California to find a new mom. I don't think he would want to drive you to the airport."

"Oh." The plan inside his head had just deflated, and it came out in his voice. His shoulders slumped as he walked away.

He isn't one to give up easily, though, and a few days later he had a better plan in mind. He had spent hours that day working on drawing something at the dining room table. "What are you working on, Titus?" I asked as I walked by.

"Oh nothin', just nothin', that's all," he said, trying to hide what he was working on.

A few minutes later he brought the paper to me. It was a map, somewhat elaborate with notes on the side. "Wow, Titus, this is a great map. You were working so hard on it. What's it for?"

"Oh, well, since you and Dad won't drive me to the airport, I'm going to ride my bike to the airport!" he stated triumphantly, jumping up and down.

"Ummm, Titus, you can't even ride your bike around our neighborhood. What makes you think you can ride your bike all the way to New York City to the airport?" I said.

"Oh, yeah. Right," he said, defeated again.

A few minutes later he was back again. "I know Mom, I'll ride my scooter to the airport instead of my bike."

"Oh, okay, but make sure you ask your sister. It is her scooter after all," I said.

"Okay, I will," he said, thumbs up.

"So, Titus, how are you going to pay for the plane ticket to California?" I asked, seeking out the rest of the plan.

"Oh, you know, the money in my piggy bank of course," he smiled.

"Titus, do you know how much it costs to fly to California?" I asked. "How much do you have in your piggy bank?"

"No, I don't know how much it costs to fly to California but I have 7 dollars and 51 cents in my piggy bank. I think that's more than enough," he said.

"Mmmm, I'm not so sure Titus. I think we need to look it up on the internet." I put aside whatever I was doing and we sat down together at the computer for a few minutes. "Well, Titus, it looks like it's going to cost about $300 for you to fly to Los Angeles, California. That is for a one-way ticket, since it sounds like you're not coming back anytime soon."

"What? $300? I don't have $300. Mom, how can I get $300?" he said.

"I think you need to get a job, Titus," I said. He slowly walked up the stairs, contemplating the next move of his escape plan.

There was no mention of his plan for the next few days. But he came to me and said sweetly, "Mom, are there any jobs I can do for you around the house?"

"Sure Titus, there are lots of jobs around the house," I replied.

"Are there any that pay $300?" he asked with excitement.

"Ummm, no Titus, there are no jobs around the house that will pay $300. You will have to do a lot of jobs to earn $300."

"Oh." he said.

"But Titus, I have a question for you. IF you do earn the $300 and you *do* find a way to get to the airport, and you *do* fly to California, who is going to pick you up at the airport?"

"Oh, that's easy, Tiffani Amber Thiessen will pick me up. She's going to be my new mom," he stated, jumping up and down, thumbs up.

I could not hold in my laughter. He was totally serious and really excited that he thought he had worked out this little detail in his plan.

"Does Tiffani Amber Thiessen know she is picking you up at the airport? Does Tiffani Amber Thiessen even know who you are? Have you ever even met Tiffani Amber Theissen or talked to her on the phone?" I asked, with serious sarcasm.

"Well no. But she will. I will take a taxi from the airport to her house! Then she will meet me and I will ask if she will be my new mom. And she will say 'Yes' because people like me, you know!" he said with confident defiance.

"Titus, you are right, people do like you. You are a nice guy. But, what if Tiffani Amber Thiessen is not a nice lady? How do you know she's nice? How do you know if she'll be a good mom to you? Does she know how to make gluten free bread for you? Does she know how to make pizza that you can eat? Does she even know how to cook? Titus, what if she says 'Go away, I don't know you.' Then what will you do?"

"But she *is* nice, Mom, she's the voice actor for Misty The Wonderful Witch in *Jake and the Neverland Pirates*. She *is* nice," he said, trying desperately to convince me.

"Okay Titus, whatever, I can't talk about it any more. I have other things I need to do today." I was getting upset, and tired of talking about the potential new mom that Titus had in mind.

Aaron had a similar, but louder, conversation with him later that night about his big plan. After that, Titus seemed to have given up about the idea. About a month later he did a rather large chore for me without being asked, and I paid him $5 in return. He proceeded to tell his dad that he was going to use the money to buy a plane ticket to California. Hearing that, I walked over and took the money right back, "You didn't tell me that you were using the money to buy a plane ticket, Titus. I want my money back. I am not helping you find a new mom."

That fall brought other big changes in our life. Over the past 6 months we had been trying to solve a housing conundrum. The house we were renting went into foreclosure soon after we moved in. We attempted to make an offer on the house, but the powers that be prevented us from doing that. So, over the summer we looked at several houses, hoping to close on one before school started. We found a great 5 bedroom house in a semi-rural area, but closing on a house took a long time, and we were unable to close until mid-October.

Our four delightful children - Fall of 2014

Along with the busyness of packing, Aaron was working very long hours, 6 or 7 days a week, 18 hour days. The kids and I rarely saw him for 4 months as he finished up a multi-million dollar contract at work. In the middle of the chaos, Aaron's car died and we decided to buy a used car and take on a car payment. With the added debt, I felt that Aaron was under too much pressure to provide all the income, so for the first time in 12 years, I decided to get a job outside the home. I was able to find a great job just minutes down the road, with decent pay, and most importantly, they were flexible with my schedule. "I need to be able to leave at a moment's notice," I stated during the interview, "If the school calls and needs me to come pick up a child, I have to be able to leave."

All the changes, mixed in with moving once again, proved to be a little much for our family. Titus' behavior escalated at home one day, and he actually hit me in anger after I had given him a consequence.

His face was red with anger as we sat face to face. He clenched his fist and hit me as hard as he could on the leg. I was shocked and didn't know what to say at first.

"Titus! You hit me! That is not okay," I said my voice shaking. "It is not okay for you to hit Mom. You go to your room." He stomped all the way up the stairs, screaming, "I wish you weren't my mom!" The door to his bedroom slammed behind him.

It was the only time he had ever hit me or anyone in our family. I was shaken. He was bigger than me now, but still had tantrums like a preschooler. I had been hoping and praying that this day would never come, the day that I was scared of my son. It scared me to think about what he was now capable of. What would this mean for his future? What would I do the next time he was angry at me? I did some praying that day, asking God for wisdom in this difficult time. After I'd calmed down a bit, I called my sister to talk about it. She is an exceptionally good listener and even better at encouraging her little sister.

Early that December, Titus made a really poor choice at school. He had the privilege of getting to go to baking class that first semester and was really enjoying it. The cupboards were, of course, filled with baking supplies and other goods used for lessons in the high school classroom. Titus had his eye on one particular item - anchovies. Titus is very much into trying new foods, and had never tried anchovies. At home, sardines were what he wanted at the time. During one session of baking class, he asked the teacher if he could try the anchovies. She told him no, of course, that she needed them for another class. The next day, however, he took the anchovies from the cupboard without asking, and hid them in the pocket of his pullover. His teachers took the anchovies away once he got back to class and wrote me a little note about the incident. When he got home I told him that I would get some anchovies for him on my next trip to the grocery store.

Apparently, that wasn't soon enough for him. During a regular counseling session his counselor attempted to talk about the incident of the previous day. "Titus, you *can't* take anchovies from the classroom without asking."

Titus immediately stood up, ran out of the room and down the hallway, pushing students out of the way, got to the baking classroom and went directly to the cupboard where the anchovies were. As he attempted to take the anchovies, the baking teacher verbally tried to stop him. Titus reacted in anger, and hit the teacher on the arm, grabbing the anchovies, "YES I CAN!" he yelled, holding the can above his head. His actions were taken very seriously by the school, of course, and he was suspended for two days.

Two days later we were in the doctor's office once again. "How has Titus's behavior been lately? Is he still doing well at home?" I shook my head and told her that Titus had hit me recently. Then that he had chosen to hit a teacher. Looking very disappointed the doctor talked to Titus. "Oh Titus. I say this to every young man because it's so important. You should *never, ever* hit a woman. Really you shouldn't hit anyone, unless you are defending yourself, but especially you shouldn't hit women. Do you understand what I mean?" "What should you do if you're angry?" "What other choices can you make?" The doctor decided to lower the dosage on his meds and within a week, his behavior was considerably better.

Later that same month, the class was scheduled to go on an outing to a play in the area, followed by lunch at a diner. Leading up to the event, Titus kept saying, "I'm going to run and run away from the group so I can do whatever I want."

The teacher called with concern in her voice. "I really would like Titus to go, but if he does run away from us, I will have to call the police. It's school policy."

I told her that I understood and that I would talk with Titus.

"Titus, I heard that you want to run away from the group tomorrow on your field trip. Is that true?" I asked.

"Who told you that? How did you find out?" he said spitefully.

"Titus, it doesn't matter who told me. Is it true? Is that your plan?" I said.

"Well, yes it is. I am going to run away from the group so that I can do whatever I want," he stated, his arms folded across his chest.

I took a deep breath, "Titus, if you run away tomorrow, you WILL NOT be going on any more field trips."

"Oh," he said, sitting down.

We chatted about it for a few more minutes. In addition to giving him an ultimatum about field trips, I also gave him some added reinforcements to think about: "Titus, IF you have an excellent morning and choose to stay with the group, you may have cheese on your burger when you get to the diner." His face brightened at the thought of a bacon cheeseburger. "And," I continued, "I have a special job for you. I think you need to hold Danielle's hand when you are walking, just to make sure that she doesn't fall on the ice. What do you think?"

"I think that's a great idea. I can do that," he said, thumbs up.

I sent him off to school the next morning with a prayer in my heart that God would keep him safe. Much to the delight of everyone, he chose to stay with the group and enjoyed a fantastic bacon cheeseburger at lunch.

Titus and I were sitting with his counselor just weeks ago during our annual transition meeting. A big, broad smile came across his handsome face: "What? Really? I get to work at the cafe?" She had just mentioned that Titus would be starting his School to Work program in the fall. His self-proclaimed dream job was working at a local internet cafe that served, among other things, gluten free items. In the past his aspirations had been working at the PEEPS factory or at a digital animation studio. But he was informed that the PEEPS factory was too far away for the bus to transport him, and that he needed to get a college degree in digital animation before he could work at Pixar. I know he'll do well at the internet cafe: what more could we have asked for as his first job? I look forward to seeing him grow and change as he enters a new season of his life, with new challenges to overcome and new people to charm with those eyes.

If I dare to look 10 years into the future, all of our other kids will be grown and off on their own adventures. Aaron and I envision that Titus will always be with us, though at some point he may choose to live in a community-like setting for people with autism. I love being a mother so much, it's comforting to think that one of my "babies" will always be close by. We will, I'm sure, have to tackle new challenges and difficult conversations along the way. One thing will never change, God never changes. He has always been with us on this path and He will continue to lead us in the future. I take solace in the fact that I don't know what the future holds for any of my children, but I know who holds the future.

Our handsome son - Fall 2014

Epilogue

There are many chapters to go in Titus' life, I've written just a few here. It's been a challenge to come to the end of this book when there are new stories to share every day, always new chapters to be penned.

I want readers to know that I am by no scale a professional on autism, nor am I a professional writer. I am, however, an expert in the life of my own son, and I have a most wonderful editor. As you may have heard, if you know one child with autism, you know one child with autism.

My memory has faded over the years. I tell my husband that part of my brain goes to each baby we've added to our family: that's why they are so smart, and I am so forgetful. That being said, there is much I have forgotten in the past 15 years or so: so many stories that didn't make it onto the pages of this book, as well as lovely people who were not even given an honorable mention. If I have forgotten a particular story, or a particular person, I apologize. My eldest son is, in fact, the memory keeper. On numerous occasions during the writing of this book, he was my calendar when I needed to remember a certain time at which an event happened. His memory is so sharp that at times he would give me the *exact date* on which an event occurred.

A perfect parent I am not. In fact, some days I feel like a complete failure, as do many women in my shoes. I am choosing to share my story, hoping that it might help just one person on the same adventurous journey as me.

APPENDIX 1

How Can You Support a Family Affected by Autism?

- Provide respite of some sort -- an afternoon, an evening, a weekend.
- Get to know the whole family; spend time with them. Families like ours crave the fellowship.
- Make a phone call just to listen, not to fix. Avoid using words like "Oh, my child does that too," or "I've been there," or "I know how you feel," -- unless of course you have. You don't have to know the right things to say, just be willing to listen.
- Take siblings of kids with autism along when your family goes for special outings or trips away. They like to feel normal too once in awhile.
- Pray for the family on a regular basis.
- Offer to watch their child while they attend a church service.
- Start an autism support group in your church or school. Most parents of autistic children don't have time to organize and run a group, but they might be willing to attend from time to time. These groups are beneficial for parents and grandparents.
- Bring over a meal -- with any dietary restrictions in mind.
- Provide allergy sensitive treats at birthday parties -- GFCF cupcakes now come in a mix that's super easy to prepare.
- Offer to take the child when their sibling has a special event and both parents would like to attend. This means so much to the whole family.

- Give your time and/or organizational skills to help them with of the loads of paperwork they have to keep track of.
- Offer invitations to coffee. Even if you think they'll say no, the offer is so appreciated.
- Invite the family over for a special meal or offer to bring a special meal and then stay -- fellowship is important.
- Unexpected visitors are often times very welcome.
- Don't be afraid to offer invitations to kids with autism -- to birthday parties, to sleepovers, to other "normal" events.

Appendix 2

Tips for Educators

- Educate your students about autism in creative ways. Find someone who's willing to come into the classroom to talk about autism generally, or even the specific child -- how to communicate best with him or her, whether or not he or she likes to be touched. Does the person have food allergies? What's it like having autism? For older kids, consider showing the movie *Temple Grandin*.

- Provide books about autism in your classroom or library.

- Provide all-inclusive programs within the school setting. Consider setting up a peer buddy system. The more kids with disabilities interact with their neurotypical peers, the better the understanding.

- Little things can set kids with autism off: desks being rearranged, new maps or bulletin boards, a clock that doesn't work, something missing from his or her desk. Give the child a warning before change occurs. "Tomorrow we are going to have an assembly."

- Post a visual schedule in the classroom, and on the student's desk.

- A timer is very helpful at home and at school.

- A communication notebook is vital for parents and teachers to share information about the child. What goes on at home will affect his day at school, and visa versa.

- Communicate with neurotypical kids: Different not less. The child with autism, or any other disability, is different than you, not less valuable than you.

- When communicating with a child with autism, use as few words as possible. Use body language and tone of voice that match your words. Kids with autism hear your words last, reading tone of voice and body language first. Teach these tips to the kids in your classroom. Role play if necessary.

APPENDIX 3

Resources

Haslem Family Links

Titus's movie: www.youtu.be/anC_PzWv_9E
Aaron's blog: http://haslemhome.blogspot.com

General Information on the Web

Relationship Development Intervention: www.RDIconnect.com

Autism Speaks: www.autismspeaks.org

Autism Awareness Association: www.autismawareness,com

Care:www.care.com - a great resource for finding respite care in your area.

National Autism Association: www.nationalautismassociation.org

Gluten Free Mama: www.glutenfreemama.com - a great website if you're looking for information and ideas in the world of gluten free eating.

A Few Favorite Blogs

https://reflectionsfromtheredcouch.wordpress.com

http://adventuresinautism.blogspot.com

Recommended Books

The Way I Feel Books - by Cornelia Maude Spelman

10 Things Every Child With Autism Wishes You Knew - by Ellen Notbohm

A Friend Like Simon - by Kate Gaynor

The Autism Acceptance Book: Being a Friend to Someone With Autism - by Ellen Sabin

Taking Care of Myself - A Healthy Hygiene, Puberty and Personal Curriculum For Young People With Autism - by Mary Wrobel

A Regular Guy - Growing Up With Autism - by Laura Shumaker

Dancing With Max - a Mother and Son Who Broke Free - by Emily Colson

Thinking in Pictures: My Life with Autism - by Temple Grandin

About the Author

Karen holds a degree in domestic engineering, and is blessed to be the mother of a child who happens to have autism. Her main purpose behind writing her personal story is to bring hope to other families on the same journey.

Karen and her husband Aaron have been married for 21 years and have 4 delightful children, ranging in age from 9 to 16. Having already resided in the states of Montana, Nevada and Oregon, they currently reside in the picturesque town of Red Hook, New York.